I0220268

permission
to practice...

Activity Journal

Your Permission to Dance Course

The Life-Changing Guide to Releasing
Self-Criticism, Letting Go of Unrealistic
Comparisons and Experiencing
the Power of Self-Love

gayla maxwell

Published in Australia by

The InsideOutcomes Group

PO Box 158, Jerrabomberra NSW 2619 Australia

connect@gaylamaxwell.com

www.gaylamaxwell.com

This book is revised version of the journal found in the back of *Permission to Dance, One Step at a Time*. Publisher InsideOutcomes Publishing House 2006.

First published in Australia 2006.

ISBN 978-0-9872286-5-9

The content in the new stand alone edition of the Permission Journal has been revised by Gayla Maxwell in 2020.

This publication is copyright and may not be resold or reproduced in any manner (except excerpts thereof for bona fide study purposes in accordance with the Copyright Act) without prior consent of the Author and Publisher.

© 2020 Gayla Maxwell

Illustrated by Mystee Unwin

Edited by Paula Wheeler

Graphic Design by Kingwell International

National Library of Australia Cataloguing-in-Publication entry

A catalogue record for this book is available from the National Library of Australia

Maxwell, Gayla

Permission to Practice: Activity Journal

1. Self-actualization (Psychology)
2. Self-esteem
3. Emotional intelligence
4. Relationships

ISBN 978-0-9872286-2-8 (paperback)

ISBN 978-0-9872286-0-4 (ebook)

Printed by Ingram Spark

Disclaimer: Every effort has been made to insure this publication is free from error or omissions. No responsibility can be accepted by the Publisher, Author or any person involved in the preparation of this publication for loss occasioned to any person acting or refraining from action as a result of material in this publication.

book signing

People have asked me if I would sign their books and I guess I've never been one for autographs myself. I never really understood the attraction. I just think it is so much more important, particularly in this book, you sign it yourself.

My signature on your book is, well it's just a signature really. My commitment to supporting your practice already exists in these pages and in my heart.

Your signature on this page however, represents your own commitment to getting the most out of the practice.

So my question to you is this: will you please sign *my* book?

Sending you love as we dance together!

Gayla.

Dear Self,

I understand the series of practices found in these pages will be nothing more than interesting at best if I read only. It is in the PRACTICING of them that I will find amazing new information about myself which leads to having greater personal power.

I am committed to being kind and light-hearted with myself as I become more aware of the opportunities that are being presented to me each day in my life.

I am committed to moving through my own unique Practice because that is how I will gain the most sustainable results.

I move forward with an open mind, a loving heart, a gentle hand and a healthy dose of laughter!

Signed: .... Date: ..../.........../...........

THE DREAM THAT STARTED IT ALL...

The dream is why I wrote *Permission to Dance* and *Permission to Practice*.

I am finally ready to share it, but never could I ignore it, nor could I forget. In fact I was never really sure it was a dream at all, or if I had somehow traveled places with the most beautiful being I'd ever seen. I still don't mind either way. I just know it changed my life.

He arrived in a space ship. Yes. It was what it was. I never got his name so I just refer to him as My Tour Guide. When I first saw him I was so drawn to his energy my feet were sliding along the ground as my body was being pulled toward him from around my solar plexus - completely out of my control. The light around him was brilliant, magnetic, and a cord of that same light connected me to him. As I got closer, about five meters away, he put his hand out to stop me, and it was like hitting a wall, minus any pain. While he never spoke a word from his mouth, I heard everything he said, mind to mind.

"You cannot come with me yet. You are not living the life you came to live. The partnership you choose is not serving you well. The smoking, and the foods you eat do not sustain your body." I had an instant knowing I was slowly wasting my life and the opportunities ahead of me. He went on to *show me* I was to eat brightly colored vegetables, reds, yellows and bright greens, in particular, beetroot, broccoli and spinach were good for me. They were all so beautiful and I could actually see the healing properties inside them. I can't explain how. I could just somehow see the atoms and the vibration of the energy which made up each vegetable. There's no other way to explain it. I didn't understand it myself.

Suddenly I was in the living room of the home where I grew up. The carpet was blue, which told me the time frame was before the renovations. My parents sat in two separate chairs with hands folded, seemingly unaware of my presence. My Tour Guide stood behind them and said telepathically, **"Remember, it wasn't your fault."** My parents divorced when I was ten years old. I knew intuitively this was what he was referring to. I couldn't remember ever thinking my parent's issues had anything at all to do with me, so this one segment stood out as strikingly unnecessary, certainly in comparison to the powerful messages in everything else I had experienced. However life was yet to unfold. He added, **"You were made perfectly. Just be you."**

In the next 'scenes' we were with some kind of 'being' I didn't recognize. I didn't really care what he was, or where we were. This gentle being held out his arm and intentionally cut it open solely for the purpose of my being witness to his healing. I was telepathically explained the science of 'cellular regeneration', but more impacting was the deep feeling of love I had in and around my body. It so intense and abundantly clear; it was the three of us standing together, forming a perfect triangle, immersed in love like I'd never known it before, and a shared clear faith in this *natural process*, which were the force causing spontaneous healing.

My Tour Guide said, LOVE is the power. It IS the power. Love heals everything you perceive to be wounded. It puts everything in right order. That is what you are doing on earth. That is the message you are meant to learn and share.

Finally one more scene. I was transported to the basement of a childhood friend's home. It was a place of joy and happiness for me growing up. It was safe. Warm. The room was filled with people dancing. There was a rhythm they all moved to together. The lights were bright and the colors more vivid than I've ever seen in my life. It was bliss. Pure joyful bliss.

My Tour Guide and I seemed to be floating above them. The joy and the colors coming off everyone filled the room so they appeared to be dancing as one. Then he said;

"Feel this. Immerse in this. Take this with you. Laugh a lot. Play forever. Practice like you cannot make a mistake. Practice Love. And always remember to give yourself Permission to Dance. That is all you really need to know."

THE DREAM UNFOLDING

I woke gasping for air, feeling as if I was reentering my body. Not sure how long I'd left it there; already wishing I could go back to be with my beautiful Tour Guide in a space ship. I felt more *at home with him* than ever had in my life.

I woke him, trying to remember all the scientific language related to something I suddenly called 'cellular regeneration' and 'spontaneous healing'; both phrases now commonly known in quantum physics, but words I'd not heard until about ten years later. My partner reminded me what time of night it was along with the "fact" that I was a little nuts, and he went back to sleep.

It was exactly two weeks and one day later when someone I knew felt a calling to share something they no longer wanted to hold inside. They said there had been a rumor for my entire life that I was quite possibly the result of an affair, and I was one of the very few who didn't know about it. I was told the father whom I had adored like he was my king, may not be my biological father at all.

For all the facts to come forward took sixteen more years because frankly, neither my dad nor I actually wanted to know. But eventually I asked for the DNA to be done, and it was confirmed. I might have been 'daddy's little girl', but I was not biologically his child. Suddenly I remembered the dream because for a moment, sixteen years later, I finally *did* wonder if my parent's divorce was because of me. **"Remember, it wasn't your fault."**

"Love heals everything you perceive to be wounded."
My dad died more suddenly than expected on June 18, 2015 of a blood clot after being aware of having bone cancer for just six weeks. It was likely he'd had it since my sister died of the same cancer seven years prior but he was blissfully unaware as he'd want it to be. A nice quick exit. No fuss about him.

When he passed it was just him and I in the hospice in the middle of the night, as it was meant to be. I got to sing him a song from his favorite Ann Murray album as he drifted away holding my hand. Only hours before on his final evening he was sitting up enjoying ice-cream and chatting away. I had asked him if there was anything he would want to tell me about life that he's learned along the way. He said, *"Yes. Nothing really matters."* I said, "You mean except maybe how well you loved?" He said, *"No. Not even that. Just be you. That is all you can ask of yourself. That's it."*

I asked my dad how he felt about dying and what does he believe will happen. He said, *"My life has pretty good but I'm ready for the next adventure."* I asked him what he thought might be in that adventure and he sort of smiled, looking extremely peaceful answering my question with a question as he often did. The last words this particularly pragmatic man would ever say to me were; **"So Gayla, do you believe in aliens?"** I finally shared my dream with him thirty years later. I couldn't help but wonder if he was going to that 'home' I saw where love is the feeling you live in and healing is natural.

I attended Camp Eden Health Spa where they showed me almost verbatim what My Tour Guide showed me about the bright vegetables. Starting in 1998 I began studies in suicide prevention, psychology, and clinical hypnotherapy which took me down this whole path of further studies on positive life choices. What sustains some to life in a way that they are able to thrive, while others struggle to survive? Who do some people find this earth easy to live on while others of us struggle? I needed to know.

In 2000 I started writing exercises for my self-esteem workshops. Laying in bed one morning it came to me; I was to collate the exercises which were helping small groups and put them in a book. I saw the words in big letters, "Permission to Dance."

"Always remember to give yourself Permission to Dance. Practice like you cannot make a mistake. Practice Love. That is all you need to know." I don't know what that 'dream' was in reality. Maybe just a dream I can't forget. Maybe a near death experience. Maybe a visitation. I honestly don't claim to understand. All I know for sure is that my life has changed because of it.

Here's to My Tour guide who helped me give myself, Permission to Dance, and Permission to Practice. I hope these pages help you do the same.

FIND OUT **WHAT'S INSIDE**

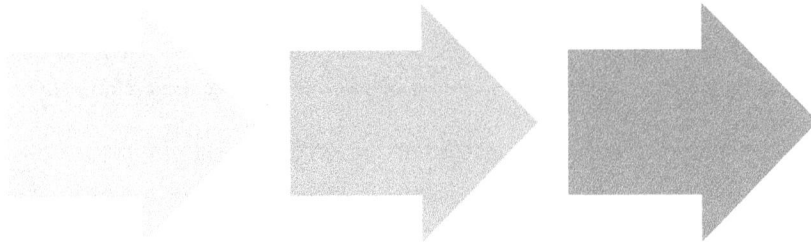

welcome

page 8

as you practice remember   10

PART **ONE**

daily reminders   **page 13**

1. i am more than I currently remember

2. i give myself permission to be self-indulgent

3. discovery takes practice and persistence and I give myself
    complete Permission to discover all I can be

4. i choose to let go of my past limitation and embrace
    the fullness of life

5. i am patient with myself and others as I feel more
    deeply and express more fully. I learn through experience.

6. i am courageous as I give myself permission feel
    the fear and do it anyway

7. i choose to find myself in good company, because I'm worth it

8. i am a work in progress…and I am all that I need to be today

9. i choose to observe the laws of the universe

10. i allow myself recovery time

11. i choose to challenge, explore and keep an open mind

PART **TWO**

the activities

page 31

1.	recreating your story	32
2.	observation vs. judgement	37
3.	judgement vs. discernment	42
4.	take responsibility and release blame	45
5.	the voices of love and fear	50
6.	replacing fear with love	59
7.	clarity comes from the inside	65
8.	you're not normal you're unique	72
9.	creating changes you really desire	89
10.	dancing on the inside	126
11.	the victim	132
12.	finding joy	139
13.	who do you think you are!?	143
14.	love and self-acceptance	148
15.	personal business plan	156
16.	personal mission statement	159

the dance is just the beginning	166
my wish for us	169
journal pages	172

WELCOME TO THE DANCE FLOOR

This *Permission to Practice Activity Journal* is a companion book to *Permission to Dance*.

I know many people are choosing to use the two books as they were designed which is to bring to life the theories, concepts and ideas i n Permission to Dance. Reading and attending seminars is great for stimulating temporary motivation. DOING SOMETHING about what you read and hear; that is what changes your life.

Some of you may not have *Permission to Dance* so it is important that you understand what our dance analogy is about. You can join a community of us all practicing together through the blogs and **www.gaylamaxwell.com** YouTube found at **www.gaylamaxwell.com**

Just to make sure we're all on the same stage together let me do a quick overview...

What IS this *Dance* thing all about?

The Dance is our analogy for *using* life and all its opportunities to discover, accept, love and contribute all that we ARE by nature...yes in that order.

Life is our **dance** floor.

Our *dance partners* are the people and the situations in our lives at any given time are the people and situations in our lives at any given time, and they offer us the opportunity to practice.

The stage or *scene* will be used in reference to what is going on at any given time in your life. You and only you have the power to change the stage because you are the main character (always) in our own dance.

We refer to *the steps* as you might think. Life is one step at a time. Practice to eventual mastery is always, *one step at a time.* I'm always fascinated how easily we humans tend to forget that.

Oh I almost forgot...when your toes get stepped on, that's when you're most likely to want to play the victim and blame your dance partner for the stuff on your stage you wish wasn't there but have yet to find the way to remove it.

And a *bruised butt* (I have to cover the complete analogy), a bruised butt is when you might want to, or may have already kicked yourself in the arsticles (my word but you understand what I mean), because you didn't live up to your own high expectations. Believe me I GET it. But it is also closely connected to wasting time feeling guilty and prolonging challenging steps you might be practicing so I suggest trying to limit the self deprivation as much as possible.

I promise it will all make a lot more sense as you begin to practice...

each morning I wake and I remember…

I have the choice to focus on joy or misery

Today, I choose to release the stories of yesterday

and I choose to give myself permission to be

truly, deeply fulfilled

What's in the journal?

Through these pages you will have the opportunity to experience and become further acquainted with your true-self filled with unlimited potential. The exercises provide ways in which you can see how your own history has played a significant part in the dances you currently attract into your life and how you might choose to create new so called 'dances' in the future.

You may discover you have been dancing to everyone's tune but your own. Don't be too surprised or tough on yourself. Most people dance to a rhythm that belongs to someone else's song until they learn more about who they are. It actually makes a lot of sense when you think about it. From childhood we only have *others* to mirror and to learn from. Gradually we learn what feels right for our own very unique journey. We discover we are different, unique and maybe a little unsure if being our true selves is completely okay!

Some people have never even known it was possible to release external influences such as what others think of them let alone given themselves permission to do so. It takes daring and know-how to change your conditioning. I can provide some of the know-how that has worked for me and many others; the courage part is all yours.

Many of the activities in the journal are focused on **observation.** Too often we are so emotionally involved in our own stories we forget that objectivity is our greatest tool for creating desirable outcomes. Without the ability to stand back and observe ourselves we can become reactive rather than proactive. We often believe the world dictates how our day is going to be, rather than taking the control seat and creating the day we desire.

Seeing our lives in the form of a dance or a story, we become more able to stand back and observe the roles we currently choose to play and with whom we act out or dance with. As we do this, we become more able to decide on the way in which we want our own story to go from here, and why we have made particular choices up until this time.

I'd like to share with you some practical ideas on how to move forward with more joy and love in your life, while letting go of the baggage that secretly keeps us bound.

As you Practice...

Use this book to the fullest so you can experience rather than just read these concepts.

Find a buddy, or many, so you can play with these ideas together. As I write the new edition final draft of this book in the midst of Covid 19, I have a team of people helping us set up the infrastructure so you can connect with one another face to face - virtually. Since the year 2000 I imagined us connecting in this way, though I couldn't have imagined the circumstance which would make it a common way to connect. USE the opportunities. It is so much easier and a lot more fun when we practice life together.

Be Active in your practice. Do at least one thing to confirm your commitment to knowing more love and happiness in your life every day. It doesn't matter if some days it seems as simple as taking a deep breath and consciously remembering to let go of anything that might limit you from being right there in that exact moment. Daily practice matters!

Be Kind. Give yourself Permission to know the kind of deep happiness that brings a smile to your face at times when you have no idea why...

Be patient with others. As you change, you change the playing field for everyone around you. They might not know today is a great day to play yet.

Be aware of attachment to judgment. It slips in so easily mostly because in our society we are so deeply programmed to judge ourselves and others. It can be a lot of fun undoing our limiting judgments especially when we do so with others who want to discover what is possible in their own lives when they too release the need to be right.

Be aware of guilt. When guilt is a repeated theme in your life, you will most certainly struggle more than you need to as you learn and grow. You've heard of the guilt trip right? Why do you think it got that connection? Guilt will make you fall down, and it can hold you down like a creeping vine around your ankles.

Laugh. Laugh often. Laugh loud. Giggle to yourself. Seriously, this whole thing of self-discovery can be a complete hoot! We are funny as we fall down and get back up over and over and over and over... I'm not suggesting you laugh at yourself, but rather with yourself. It is my goal to show people how they can enjoy the process of discovery even more than the discoveries themselves!

Connect with others

If I could say there is one single most important aspect to learning to know real love and deep happiness in our lives, I would have to say it would be to connect in an authentic manner with others. Okay I know people who argue that with me. Sure I get that nature, animals, and every other aspect of the universe all provide an opportunity to witness ourselves in relationship to our surrounds. However for most of us nothing can press our buttons nor feels as good as another living human being. We find out how we're doing with this whole 'love & happiness' thing as we allow people to love us and/or push our buttons. From business relationships to lovers, parents, children, ex-partners, shop assistants, bus drivers, and the parking ticket attendant...connect.

EACH DAY I REMEMBER...

WHAT I THINK MATTERS

WHAT I SAY MATTERS

WHAT I DO MATTERS

I MATTER.

Some things to remember, over and over and **OVER** again...

You might discover I repeat myself. Know why? Because that's life. Life just keeps repeating the same messages over and over and over again until we graduate to the next message, which of course will also play out over and over and over again. Know why? Because we forget.

That was one of, (amoungst several) lessons I didn't actually take to all that kindly, however once I accepted it, life got a lot easier.

So with that in mind, I'm more than happy to share with you a few shortcuts. I've listed eleven things that are easy to forget , yet are essential to ongoing commitment to giving ourselves permission to grow-up guilt free and have the life we came here to live.

I am more than I currently remember

We are all *more* than we can possibly imagine, regardless of how many self-help courses and/or books we have absorbed, or how many years of therapy we have or have not undergone.

If there was nothing left to discover about who we are, what would be the point of this whole exercise called *life?* Surely we could be somewhere else…a place where everyone admires and respects everyone else and lives in complete harmony, each person contributing their natural gifts! I'm sure that's where I'd choose to be if I didn't have a few more lessons to learn.

2

I give myself Permission to be healthfully self-indulgent!

It is the kindest thing you can do for the world. As we allow ourselves to be all that we are, we give others Permission to do the same. We will naturally feel less judgmental toward others as we understand our own need to live life in accordance with our true selves. Others may not always like it. That has nothing to do with us. In fact it is none of our business! It is part of their journey, their judgment and their choice to give away their power to someone else's life.

When we are true to our own greatest intention we not only serve ourselves, we are being the perfect dance partner in the bigger picture. We may not always know how. Sometimes it isn't necessary to know, so we're not shown. Other times we are given the blessing of seeing how our seemingly self-centered actions benefited another process that did not seem connected to us. We are all connected. So take loving care of yourself.

In healthy self-indulgence we find our unique offering

Supporting the unveiling of what any one person has to offer our collective earth family is probably one of my life's greatest passions. Each time a client, friend, associate or someone in my family unveils a new layer and becomes more aware of the many gifts that make them who they are, I suddenly know feelings I have yet to find words suitable to express. Gratitude, excitement and joy all seem to be dull words compared to the emotions I experience. I am aware of the courage it required for them to give themselves Permission to be self-indulgent.

This book is a result of my own healthy self-indulgence.

If I had not been willing to submerge into myself, I would never have discovered the very specific gifts I can offer. I started writing because I had a burning desire to do so. Five years later, I discovered that by fulfilling my own desire, I have something very specific to offer and if I had not had been so self-indulgent, nobody else could have written this book—at least not exactly as I have.

As we explore our uniqueness with less judgment and more freedom, we not only find the true joy that hides in giving ourselves Permission to be all that we are (though that is wonderful in itself!), we also discover more of what it is we must share with others. Together we become more.

As you write in your journal and do the exercises, immerse yourself in them like nobody is watching. Indulge yourself! It is your life story and you write the book. Enjoy each page!

If you look up "self-satisfaction" in the thesaurus, you will find such matching words as complacency, smugness, conceit, vanity, superiority, and narcissism. Oh my! We need to re-write that book! Anyone got the urge? Anyone at all?

"Self-indulgence" is even more interesting! The act of allowing ourselves to reach out for what we desire is matched with such words as hedonism, decadence and self-pity.

I want to make it clear that in the context of this book, the words self-indulgent simply mean to allow oneself to feel satisfied and fulfilled in accordance with our soul's highest vision for what is rightfully, naturally and lovingly ours. If in our society it is considered to be vain, conceited and/or smug to have self-satisfaction and to indulge ourselves in our spirit's wildest desires, it is no wonder we have so much difficulty justifying our need for peace, time out, love and the like, much less allowing ourselves permission to go out and get it!

To be "self-centered" in the context of the Permission philosophy simply means to be centered in spirit and therefore inspired to support the highest vision of the grandest version of your true-self. If this appears to be selfish by others' standards, it is none of our business.

3

Discovery takes practice and persistence and I give myself complete Permission to discover all I can be

Every good scientist knows the discovery of something useful is based on many more discoveries of something not useful. They just continue to discover what doesn't work, eliminate that factor, and try something else.

Through doing the exercises in this journal and allowing them to be a part of your daily practice, you gradually open up the opportunity to rediscover some of the more hidden parts of yourself that are powerful. You may also discover the parts of yourself that are no longer useful to you. These may come in the form of negative old beliefs, hurtful behavior and/or self-destructive thoughts. It is this experimentation with life that can raise your awareness and help you find what is useful to you, while losing what has been sabotaging your ability to know true love.

I choose to let go of my past limitation and embrace the fullness of life

As you bring the unconscious or hidden beliefs into the light of consciousness you can then decide with greater clarity whether these beliefs hinder or support your life now. When you were a child you might have decided to protect yourself from pain because you felt, for whatever reason, you had to do so for survival. You might have believed you were unsafe in some way then and have carried these subconscious beliefs into the present. Now you find yourself unable to trust, fall in love, commit, stay connected, or a multitude of other outcomes resulting from subconsciously believing you are in some way unsafe.

Children process incoming information much more simplistically than adults, yet there is a part within each of us who is still that child. In fact today, in this moment, we are still all that we have ever been, child, adolescent, and adult.

Our cells store every piece of information that has crossed our path. Experiences we would call *good* or *healing* and the more painful experiences are subconsciously guiding the way we interpret life today.

5

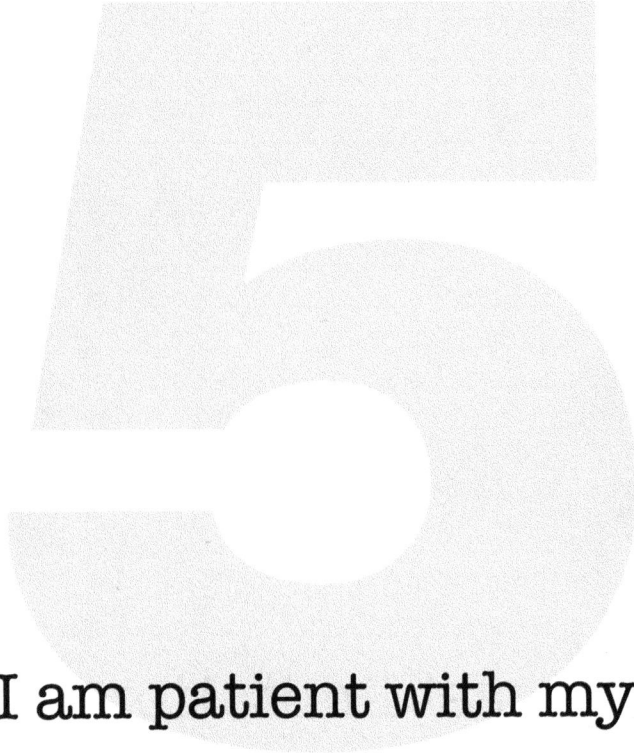

I am patient with myself and others as I feel more deeply and I learn through experience

Sustainable and true healing does not occur through having an intellectual understanding. Rather, it occurs naturally as we give ourselves permission to feel and let go.

Through my own process of waking up to who I really am, I became extremely frustrated with myself as I continued to repeat behavior that was non-productive and self-sabotaging. I wondered what was wrong with me given all that I knew about emotional wellbeing. I thought I had done it all! I read all the books, I kept a journal, I left my country of birth so as to have my own life, I cried, I talked about things until my mouth was dry and the listener's ears were red! I had heard the stories and had some memory of my childhood. Some of it was tough. So what? Everyone has a story. In my line of work, which at the time was suicide prevention, I knew that many people had much sadder stories than mine.

I would wonder why I continued to struggle repeatedly with the same things when I believed my healing was complete in a particular area. I was to discover that while I had an intellectual understanding; I never really allowed myself permission to feel the wounds that were inflicted behind the stories. Everyone has them. Mine needed some attention.

Then I decided to study clinical hypnotherapy. Believe me, when you study anything to do with emotional wellbeing, before you know it you become the client, a lot! Daily role play therapy whether you thought you needed it or not. (Most of us did!)

My teachers were not at all fooled by the participant's previous studies and wealth of knowledge, in fact our intellectual armor and spiritual gaga were thrown out the window within five minutes of day one in class.

If we were to authentically connect with our future clients, we would first have to become aware of our own need to heal the subconscious blocks we were carrying ourselves.

Fun Fact: Our behaviors are not based on what we think we believe, but rather what we have 'safely' tucked away in the pockets of our neurology. Our negative or sabotaging thoughts, feelings and behaviors make a whole lot more sense when we start looking into those little cheeky pockets and we discover the child we once were who is unfortunately running the show.

I initially argued I had a healthy self esteem; the adult me was absolutely clear I was worthy of unconditional love, but the child within me had yet to have it proven to her.

Fun Fact #2; It is quite natural to move away from pain and seek pleasure. It is human instinct.

Unfortunately when it comes to emotional healing, what we subconsciously believe to be pain, is more often than not, a harmless childhood belief, and it the key to our freedom. We tend to go around the wounds by intellectualizing rather than going *through* them by allowing ourselves to feel the fear and get to the other side. We do this in order to 'protect' ourselves from pain.

The moving through emotion technique I practice is an amazingly simple process. I now practice it as a way of life, and I share it with my clients who are just as surprized as I was when I learned, we can let go of any emotion quite effortlessly when we know how.

Fun Fact #3: Did you know you physically cannot stay in any emotion for more than about ten seconds? Really! If we just let ourselves absolutely immerse in whatever emotion comes up, and we didn't continue to 'think' about what's causing it, but rather we just feel it, the feeling will morph into another feeling! Once we identify that feeling, it morphs also; and so it continues. Until we have nothing left but a feeling of peace.

How we manage to achieve staying in any emotion longer than ten seconds is by feeding our neurons the same story that got us into the feeling in the first place. We go into a loop, which feeds the emotion.

I do this guided technique with my clients and I can assure you, ten seconds actually feels a long time when you give yourself absolute permission to feel any particular emotion as intensively as you can - AND YOU FOCUS ON INTENSIFYING THE FEELING, NOT THE STORY; naturally it shifts.

More commonly however, our egos are telling us that fueling the justification for being angry, hurt, stuck or whatever limiting emotion we feel, is best served by numbing ourselves. Alcohol, drugs, keeping busy, being around people who do not give us permission to feel, and/or people who allow us to wallow in our sad story—these are all tricks to keep us from moving through and discovering what is possible in our lives. What is living just on the other side of our self-sabotage?

As we master the skill of feeling in order to let go, we become more able to deal with whatever is happening around us at the time. We learn how to experience and then let go. That's not to suggest nobody will ever be able to hurt you again, but it is suggesting you will be more equipped to move through it with greater ease.

Be patient with yourself as you learn the power hidden within your emotions.

TIME TO STOP THINKING AND TALKING
...TAKE ACTION!

I am not a big believer in the idea we need to analyze every situation large and small, taking 18 months in therapy to engage in this process, telling the same story over and over again. I do believe we need to give space to our feelings *behind* the story and in any moment where they arise. Emotional release is a tool we can use at any time as we live our day-to-day lives. (See exercise 1a *Recreating Your Story*). If you need help to get into this part of your journey, please allow your own guidance to lead you to where you're meant to find it.

Intellectualizing or mentally understanding an issue is the easy part. In fact, it is often where so many people get stuck. They repeat their story, the issues, the fears and the blockages they feel, week after week to their therapist (or whomever will listen). Unfortunately staying stuck in the story serves the ego's desire to confirm they really are very stuck and it will be difficult to change the nasty mess that is their life.

This constant telling of the story might serve to help the individual's intellectual understanding of their pain but they are often left with the question: What else do I have to learn in order to let it go of the painful patterns once and for all? The most probable short answer to that question is *nothing*. There is very likely nothing left to learn from the intellectualizing; however, there is certainly more to experience. And it is experience that takes us past the intellectual understanding phase of healing.

We must find the courage, the trust, and allow ourselves the Permission to move from a place of thinking to a place of feeling and finally, letting go.

As we become more spiritual in our understanding without equally allowing ourselves to be physical, we can lose sight of the fact we are human. And as humans, we will feel pain, anger, hurt, irritation and all of the many emotions that make up the human experience. We were not only blessed with the happy emotions, we were blessed also with the emotions that remind us we are human after all!

Sometimes this fact can make the most God-loving individual appear to be a raving lunatic. (And yes, I do have some firsthand experience here.) So be it. At our essence, we are still only love. We just need to explore the part of ourselves that is temporarily unable to feel that love so we can reconnect to it. It is like shining love Light onto pained darkness. As we do this, the pain can no longer stay hidden.

6

I am courageous as I give myself permission feel the fear and do it anyway

The journey of conscious discovery is as exciting as it is challenging. There truly is *nothing to fear but fear itself.* We are only in fear of the Boogie Man that we believe is hiding under the bed. He doesn't exist. He didn't exist when you were little, and he doesn't exist now. But he certainly can feel very real and very debilitating in the child part of our minds.

As you look under the bed, recognizing the ideas and beliefs that no longer serve you, you are given the opportunity to clean out whatever hides in the darkness. As you embrace the Boogie Man, you set yourself free. (He could probably use a good hug anyway—Can you imagine having *his* reputation?)

7

I choose to find myself in good company, because I'm worth it

Find yourself often in the company of those with whom you feel comfortable in being the many complex and simple shades and colors of yourself. Each interaction is a mirror reflection of who you are. It is important therefore to create balance—seeing yourself through other's loving, kind and supportive eyes. This is as much a representation of who you are as is the fearful part of you. Find yourself in the eyes of love. There will be plenty of opportunities to see a mirror reflection of how you look in fear. We certainly need not go out looking for it! Allow yourself to be nurtured by those who love you. As you receive love, you give others the opportunity to share their gifts—and you allow yourself to be human.

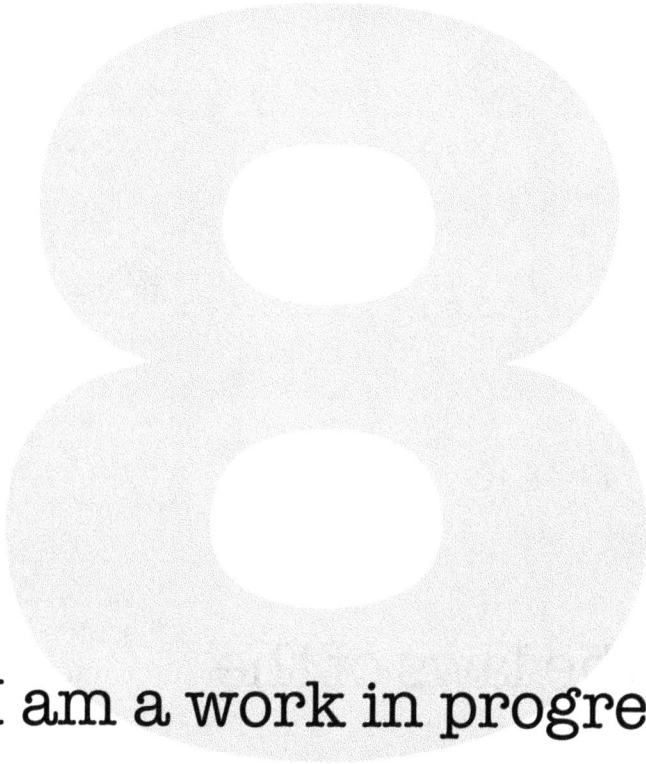

I am a work in progress...
and I am all that I need to be today

There is little point to pretending to be or feel something just because it seems to be the *spiritual*, the *strong* or the *nice* thing to do. It is not in line with your own integrity. It does not serve your dance and most importantly, you cannot trick universal law.

If you feel the struggle, that's really okay. It means you are a work in progress like the rest of us and you're choosing the road less traveled. You are enough even in the moments you are dancing in your darkness. Just be aware, be kind and keep being you.

I choose to observe the laws of the universe

I often relate our personal discovery to the laws that apply to discoveries in the scientific world. While there is no right or wrong way scientists must make their discoveries, in the end *there is that which works to support their desired discovery and that which does not*. They start with a hypothesis (a thought or belief) and they proceed to experiment by exploring what they suspect might prove their hypothesis to be correct. Gradually, by process of elimination and many "unexpected" discoveries, they prove or disprove their theory.

As we discover our own unique essence we go through the very same process. We think or believe things about ourselves and we set out to prove them to be true. We might believe we are unworthy of unconditional love and then call in every opportunity to validate the theory. However, along the way, just like the scientist, we discover so much more than the proving or disproving of our original theory. We discover also who we are not. And we discover what works for us, what makes us feel peaceful, safe, happy, comfortable, and motivated, and what feels binding, limiting, chaotic and intense. While all things can be used to support the gathering of information as we "experiment," some people and situations serve only to provide a detour, the long way or a mirror image of who we do not want to be.

When I don't like the way things are going in my life and I am living in ways that do not work for me, like any good scientist I go back to the basics and I ask myself a few questions to solve the problem. I head it up like this:

It happens every time...	When it isn't working for me I observe why:
What I give out I get back.	Am I happy with what I'm putting out to the world? Am I being honest with myself about my intentions?
The people and situations in my life are mirrors that help me see aspects of myself.	Am I happy with what I'm putting out to the world? Are they showing me aspects of who I am or aspects of who I am not? What buttons are being pushed for me?
If I am not coming from a loving space	What is the fear I attach to this person or situation? What do I need to do differently, right this minute, to get back to my center?
What I focus on grows (and usually becomes my reality!)	Am I focusing on thoughts and actions that will support or pull me away from my highest purpose? Is my focus on love or fear?
The more time I spend with people and situations that support my loving discoveries, the easier it is to center myself in love.	How and with whom am I spending my time? Am I allowing myself space to grow? Am I practicing any centering techniques such as yoga or meditation? Am I counterbalancing challenging people and situations with a healthy dose of self-nurturing?

As I honor myself in this way,
I gain more opportunities to see
myself being the loving person
I naturally am.

I allow myself recovery time

Each one of these exercises is a collection of my own recoveries as I clumsily learned to give myself *Permission to Dance* in my own unique way. Each time I fell down or tripped over my own feet or someone else's, I had to find a way to get back up to be stronger, more knowledgeable, and never bitter from the fall. I call this process of getting back up *my recoveries.*

Take time to recover with each clumsy trip over your own two feet. Lick your wounds, laugh at yourself, have a warm cup of tea…and get your butt back up onto that dance floor!

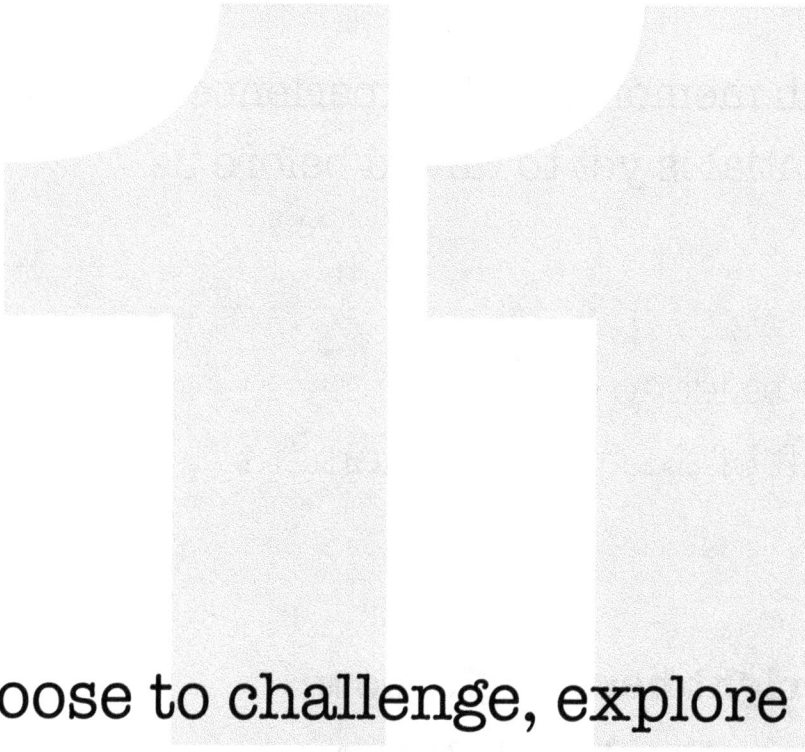

I choose to challenge, explore and keep an open mind

I invite you to explore and uncover all the many interesting and exciting facets of who you are as you share this journey of discovery. I encourage you to challenge the ideas presented all the way throughout this book. Play, ask others how they feel, meditate on the ideas, read other material on these topics. In this way *you* decide what feels right for you and what doesn't…all the while unveiling who you are at the core.

An open mind allows for new information to be processed. A closed mind remains without knowledge. Wouldn't the world be a very different place if Albert Einstein and Thomas Edison chose ignorance?

May you find greater love and compassion for yourself and for our collective family as you gently awaken and discover the true love and power that is within you.

I am a child, an adolescent;
I am the youthful and I am who I am right now
I am more than you or I can see today

for I carry each memory, each experience in my heart
while my potential is yet to unfold before us

Today I choose to let go of any history
limiting the gift of this present moment

**For it is only right here, right now
I can experience the deep fulfillment
of life's promise**

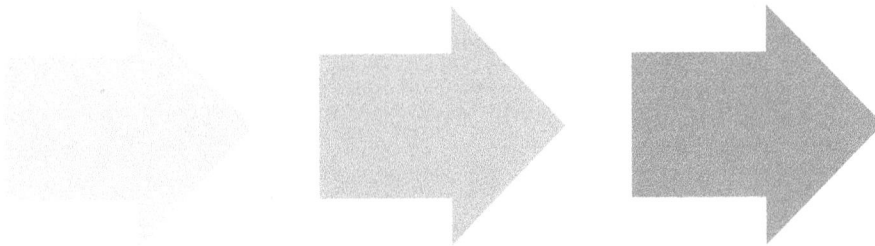

ACTIVITIES
ACTIVITIES
ACTIVITIES
ACTIVITIES
ACTIVITIES
ACTIVITIES
ACTIVITIES
ACTIVITIES
ACTIVITIES
ACTIVITIES

1. Recreating Your Story

Opportunity to Experience Yourself as Your Own Greatest Companion

The following exercise offers an opportunity for you to practice being your own greatest companion. It is important you do the entire exercise and not leave it half completed. I suggest you allow a minimum of half an hour per individual experience to you give yourself time to do the whole process. (Take longer if you feel like it.)

Addressing one experience at a time is enough. You may choose to do more; however, the key to using this *Practice Journal* most effectively is to work through it steadily rather than going hard at the beginning, bombarding yourself with too much information and too much pressure to "fix" yourself. *Permission* aims to make the *process* more enjoyable and more loving rather than promising ten steps to a quick fix. (To my knowledge there isn't one or I promise you I would have included it.)

Enjoy the journey and trust that an amazing destination awaits you. It is all unfolding in perfect order.

Sharing the Experience

You may also choose to have someone do the exercise with you. I would suggest if you do this, you choose someone you trust to have your highest good at heart. You may have a good friend, a family member, a therapist or counselor who might be happy to support this process also. I would only suggest you choose wisely whom you share with. This is your life experience, and each moment should be honored.

Revisiting the story, unveiling the feeling

Throughout our lives we have all experienced pain in one form or another. While this in itself is neither good nor bad (all experience being useful), if we were too young or unaware of how to process the experience in a way that was supportive, as we have already learned, it is likely to leave us with subconscious beliefs and behavior that no longer serve our adult life today.

This is the opportunity for you to tell your story and recreate it as you would have preferred it played out. Use the space below to write in, or get a voice recorder if you don't like writing—either way, get your story out. We're going to start as early as you can remember and year by year, memory by memory, move into the present.

You will find in Exercise 1B there is only one space but please use your own journal or the back pages of this one to add as many 'stories' about your childhood as come up for you.

EXERCISE 1A

MY FAMILY

1. Position in the family (eldest, adopted, the fifth child of seven, etc.)

2. Your feelings about your position in the family and why?

3. My early childhood relationship with parents/guardians was:

In all cases under the family heading, include your feelings as you remember them surrounding these relationships.

4. My adolescent relationship with parents/primary adolescent care providers:

5. My current relationship with these people:

EXERCISE 1B

MY EXPERIENCES #1

1. The earliest fearful or unhappy experience I can remember was when I was_____years old. I remember:

    Describe details of the story.

2. I remember feeling:

    Write as much detail about your feelings as possible. How did you feel about the smells, the sounds,
    the environment, and what was going on around you?

3. If I could have rewritten the script, I would:

    You may have had an unmet need such as the need for more reassurance, love, nurturing,
    etcetera. Rewrite the story as it would have been in your image of the perfect childhood world.

4. If I could have loved that child then as I would love an innocent child now that I am an adult, I would have:

What would you have done to reassure or to love that child exactly as he/she needed to be loved at the time? Be specific.

5. Sit with your response:

Close your eyes and see that child, you. See her/him in front of you, (the adult) and allow these two parts of yourself to experience unconditional love. Feel it. Try not to move away from it. Just allow yourself to cry if you feel like crying. Laugh if you feel like laughing. No judgment. Just be present with your emotions.

6. When you feel you have come to the natural close of that experience, see this child becoming smaller and smaller so he/she fits in your hand. Gently put the child, you, in an imaginary pocket close to your heart and where you can bring him/her out whenever you choose.

The next time in your day-to-day life that you feel the same feelings as you described above in number two, check-in with the child inside. Close your eyes and imagine bringing that child back out of your pocket and asking what she/he needs from you. When you are acting out in fearful ways, you will usually discover that a part of you is still stuck in a past emotional experience.

By allowing this part of yourself to be heard, you acknowledge and accept a greater part of who you are. This way you can gradually mesh all the many parts, the many ages and the many experiences that make up you.

Notes:

Repeat this exercise as often with as many ages and experiences as you can. This may take you weeks, months or years to get through if you so choose. It is an exercise you can keep coming back to as you become more comfortable with learning how to self nurture.

You need not stay on this activity if you wish to move forward, however, I recommend that you go through this process at least with one age/experience before moving on.

Use this exercise whenever you feel the need to bring a part of yourself, an age, or a personality relating to that age into the foreground. She/he will be grateful for the opportunity to be loved—especially by you!

The only purpose for remembering the past is to GROW from it.

You may find as you recognize yourself to be the powerful and capable person you are today, you might want to give a little more of that strength and love to the child within you who still reaches out for more.

What so many people are doing unconsciously is further abusing the child who is desperately trying to be heard. The emotionally wounded part of you will act out through temper tantrums, insecurities, frustrations and every other way that fear expresses itself. When one of your buttons is pressed, you can be sure there is a message in there somewhere for you. (I did say *the message is FOR YOU,* not the other person! What they have to deal with is their business, remember?)

Remember you can revisit this exercise many times over.

Notes:

2. observation vs. judgment

Observation without Judgment = the Unveiling of Discernment

I am not the behavior nor the relationship

I am not my skin nor my clothes size

I am the part within that is never changing

I am the spectator

As I watch my own life and the choices I make

I observe my own creation

And awaken the discernment that is my knowing.

If you are to move into the fullness of your authentic, loving and empowered self, you must first observe without judgment where you are today; then decide where you want to be, and proceed in love to fill the gap. I do not refer to how much money you would like to earn or how you would like to fill your days. I refer to how you want to feel, think and behave in your own life. These are the three things we inevitably wish to change. How we feel, how we think and how we behave—each one affecting the others.

Your world is what you perceive it to be.

Starting today, we're going to practice seeing things just as they are, rather than deciding whether this is good, bad, right or wrong. Practice opening your mind to the opportunities that come from all that is in your world in any given moment.

EXERCISE 2A

OPPORTUNITY TO PRACTICE NON-JUDGMENT

1. Look around the room you are in. Look at the colors you like, (minimum of three colors) and for each color say the following statement:

    The color_____is neither a good color nor a bad color. I simply feel drawn to it in this moment. Other people may or may not feel drawn to this color. You may not be drawn to it tomorrow. Just be in this moment.

2. *Look at the individual items* you particularly like (at least three things) and say:

    This_____is neither good nor bad. I am simply attracted to it. Others may, or may not be attracted to it. I may not be tomorrow. Today I simply observe this _____.

3. Look at the books you have enjoyed reading and say:

    This book is neither good nor bad, I simply enjoyed reading it. Others may or may not. Today I simply observe the books I've read.

EXERCISE 2B

NON-JUDGMENT IN PRIMARY RELATIONSHIPS

Now we're going to take it one step further as we look at the **primary relationships★** you currently have in your life.

The relationship I have with my (include each person's relationship to you as well as his or her name) is not a good or bad relationship. It is a generous opportunity for me to know myself more intimately.

Repeat this sentence until you have exhausted your list of primary relationships.

This is a simple one-minute exercise you can do whenever you are feeling judgmental about your relationships and the people within them! Very often it is the people who contribute the most to our unveiling who we judge the most harshly.

★ Primary relationships are those with parents, children, siblings, significant others.

When the words in the above affirmation came through me, I was profoundly affected by their meaning. The words, "a generous opportunity to know myself more intimately" stuck in my head. When I really thought about it, I realized the magnitude of the implications of another person's life being used so I could know myself more intimately. It certainly puts a whole different slant on everything from war to the everyday disagreement doesn't it?

Take a moment to pause here. Think about it. In fact take an hour, a day, or a week! This concept takes a great deal of practice in order to embrace so if it's only serving to frustrate you today, explore your frustration.

Challenge this idea of nothing being good or bad. Debate it with friends. Explore its possibilities.

EXERCISE 2C

OBSERVE GRATITUDE

When I practiced this idea of things being neither good nor bad, gradually seeing how all things can be used to serve my greater understanding, I suddenly felt quite overwhelmed with gratitude, in particular for my mother, with whom I've had a challenging relationship for many years. I picked up the telephone to call her in Canada the moment *I got it*. I realized I no longer had to hold onto the pain I had associated with our relationship. I could now rejoice in her offering—one of which stood out so profoundly. She allowed her life to be used in order to give me mine!

Give yourself a moment to think about a situation that is challenging to you. See if you can find a reason to feel grateful for its offering to your life.

EXERCISE 2D

NON-JUDGMENT IN CHALLENGING SITUATIONS

Finally, focus on situations or *stories* going on in your life that currently challenge you (minimum of three). Describe briefly the situation followed by the phrase that follows:

Challenge 1

is not a good thing or a bad thing, it is simply an opportunity for me to experience myself and observe how I feel in relation to it.

Challenge 2

is not a good thing or a bad thing, it is simply an opportunity for me to experience myself and observe how I feel in relation to it.

Challenge 3

is not a good thing or a bad thing, it is simply an opportunity for me to experience myself and observe how I feel in relation to it.

As we rid our perception of judgment about ourselves and others, we discover a world that is less stressful and distinctly more peaceful. It is interesting to observe how much time and effort we spend putting pressure on ourselves to have an opinion, to judge and to analyze situations.

Most people think judgment or analysis is a form of protection from the fear of the unknown. They believe if they don't decide by analysis what is good or bad, they become vulnerable and therefore weak. However, I've found that nothing could be further from the truth. It is our judgment, which creates fear and fear, which creates judgment.

EXERCISE 2E

OPPORTUNITY TO PRACTICE NON-JUDGMENT IN YOUR DAY-TO-DAY LIFE

As a thought comes into your head, simply be aware of it and let it pass. It is not good or bad, it just is. As a situation occurs, it is not good or bad, it just is. As you meet with people during your day, they are not good or bad, or right or wrong, they just are—based on your own point of reference.

Example:

As you get a series of red lights on your way to work when you are already running late, simply observe your feelings, your thoughts and the situation as it is. Resist the urge to judge yourself as you practice.

As you come to a red light you would say something such as, "This red light has no meaning but that which I give it." Or, "I am not good or bad at this exercise, I'm just doing it."

While it might seem like you're kidding yourself at first, just keep practicing each day this week. If you don't already, you will soon agree everything is an opportunity to practice and know yourself more intimately.

There is no moment in your day that cannot be used to practice this exercise, but I recommend you limit yourself to only four focused practice sessions on your first day, each session being a minimum of one minute.

This brings you to a total of four minutes required of you today. Can you commit that much time to yourself?

Carry this journal or a notepad with you and record your observations:

3. judgment vs. discernment

I am often asked how one can survive in this world without having judgment. How will we know if we should take the job, marry the man/woman, befriend the person or move toward any new experience? How will we know what is right or wrong, good or bad for us if we don't judge the information presented?

The first part of the answer is painfully repetitive and consistent, (as I'm told I can be!)

"There is no right or wrong experience, only that which will serve your highest purpose and that which will not. ALL can be useful even the detours.

The second part of my answer relates to *discernment*.

It is important to understand the difference between *judgment* and *discernment* and that both are available to us in any given moment. Judgment is born of the ego's need to limit us. The trick is this: If the ego (the master of fear), can bog us down in details, drama and the stories of our lives, it gains power to limit us from knowing our real ability to simply *know* where to be, for how long and when. We know.

If we are stuck in *he said, she said* and our perception that *our judgment is the right one*, we are coming from a limited viewpoint (which is always a by-product of one fear or another). In this way we stay disconnected or blocked from the part of our self that has great discernment.

While we are working toward removing our ego's controlling habitual need for judgment, we gradually learn to accept our growing sense of discernment that naturally replaces it.

Discernment is of the Soul

To be discerning by dictionary definition is "to be astute, acute, clear-sighted, (otherwise known as clairvoyant), clear-knowing, (claircognisant) perceptive, (intuitive), sensitive (clairsentient) and wise."

The more connected we are to that part within us that is the witness, the unchanging or the essence of our true selves, the more the gift of intuition becomes available to us. We gain a greater awareness of what works in our lives and what might serve us better to avoid. Some refer to this as "listening to their gut".

If a person, a place or situation is not supportive of your soul's advancement, discernment allows us to remove ourselves from getting caught up in the story and the judgment of the situation; we simply move away gently, without the drama that judgment causes.

When unsure if you are coming from

Love (discernment)

or FEAR (judgment)

Check on your clarity levels

Chaos and Confusion are always

by-products of the EGO (fear)

Calmness and Clarity

are always by-products of SPIRIT (love)

If you don't know what to do try doing NOTHING

Sometimes stillness is all that is required

EXERCISE 3A

OPPORTUNITY TO PRACTICE DISCERNMENT

1. Observe your thoughts and your inner voices. Pay attention to both the voice of love and the voice of fear. Try not to judge, but simply take note, regardless of which voice it is.

    General observations:
    Today I noticed I have been thinking:

    Some obvious thoughts that relate to my voice of love:

    Some of the more obvious thoughts that came from my ego:

actions speak louder than words...
but the words in our head will determine our actions.

Our actions will determine outcomes

Let the voices run wild and get ready for chaos!

4. take responsibility… release the need to blame

EXERCISE 4A

OPPORTUNITY TO BECOME MORE SELF-RESPONSIVE

When we blame others or a situation for the story we ourselves co-create with our many dance partners, we are often more prone to feelings of frustration, anger, hatred and so on.

Remind yourself that as you observe your ego's contribution, it is only a part of yourself that still needs healing. It is easy to become judgmental of yourself as you recognize the ways in which you have *not* been taking responsibility.

The flip side of this of course is avoiding this exercise all together because you are unwilling to look at how you contribute to the situations and relationships in your life that are not working as well as they could. "It isn't my fault! If only he was…then I would be fine!" The reason some people will find this one difficult is that to take responsibility for their actions equates to taking the blame. Seeing where we are playing a part that does not serve us any longer is not about taking the blame, it is simply an opportunity to grow.

If we let go of the word **blame** and replace it with, **I take responsibility for my contribution,** that's a great start.

1. Take responsibility for feelings of frustration. Try to describe an interaction or situation you experienced this week that "caused" you to react with the feeling of frustration or anger. Try to include as much detail as possible:

   *(Give us all the **he said she said** stuff that will soon be off limits in your training to become more self empowered!)*

2. The feelings behind the interaction/situation:

3.   **Anger and Frustration = Fear.** Identify what it is that you feared in this case:

4.   How did you act out this fear? (guilt, sarcasm, angry words, anger, kept to yourself, etcetera)

5.   If you are able to, briefly identify why you might have this particular fear. Sit quietly with the question; take a deep breath and trust. Listen more to how you feel than what you think. Your ego wants to keep you analyzing in your head. Your place of true knowing is in your heart, your gut, your Spirit. As you breathe, try to take your focus down into your body rather than up into your head. If nothing comes, let it go. If feelings do arise, write them down after allowing yourself space to feel them.

6.   Go into the fear more deeply with the intention of releasing and letting go of the control this feeling had over us in the past. Trust that you are in control, not the feeling. It is merely there to tell you something within you needs more love. Record any thoughts or feelings for later reflection. It's wonderful to look back in later times and observe what you have had the courage and strength to heal.

EXERCISE 4B

INNER CHILD VISUALIZATION

Permission to Let Go . . . one breath at a time CD activity

If you *do* have the *Permission to Let Go* CD, you might choose to listen to the "Inner Child" guided visualization today (found on track 3) and answer the questions that follow.

If you *do not* have the *Permission to Let Go* CD, this is a good time to revisit exercise 1a–b that relates to your Inner Child experiences. Continue to visualize or imagine yourself as the small child and ask her/him what she needs in order to feel loved unconditionally.

1. Following the Inner Child guided visualization I felt:

2. These are my observations about the parts of myself that act out defensively, in anger, frustration, withdrawal, or any other way in which I might try to protect myself from others:

3. Ask your inner child (the part of you that still feels hurt from childhood), **"What is it that you need to help you feel safe, loved and without fear. What do you want from me in order to heal?"**

4. Close your eyes again for about 30 seconds or until you have been able to see, feel, hear or imagine your inner child. Take a deep breath and visualize, imagine the small child in the palm of your hand. (You may even choose to physically put your hand out.) Look into the face of this little person... And **feel.**

5. Open your eyes and write the first words that come to you. *Use the hand you do not normally write with.*

As I choose to let go of my perceived limitations

I allow myself to become a more positive
and powerful person

The world is in need of more of us!

**Not everyone is willing to find the courage to give
themselves "permission" to be all that they are …**

But I am!

Keep remembering to pat yourself on the back for the small steps.
Don't wait for someone else to do it.
This is just another way in which you take responsibility for yourself.

5. the voices of love and fear

As you move through this time of awakening to your own unique dance, it is important to watch **your language!**

Your inner voice of fear does not appreciate your choice to see the world through more awakened, and therefore more powerful, non-judging eyes. You are likely to find as you practice remembering who you are, your inner voice could be telling you all kinds of untruths about whether or not you are succeeding.

The Familiar Language of the Ego (Fear) Voice:

- I know better than to believe this (loving) garbage

- That (thought/action) wasn't very nice. See? I'm not a nice person.

- I will never change

- Nothing ever changes

- I have too much baggage to really move forward

- If people knew what I know about myself they wouldn't like me either!

- I am just stuck with what I've got

- I can't

- I'm too (anything)

- I'm not enough (in any way)

- I am not good enough

Another sure sign our ego voice is talking is when we hear words such as should, have to, bad, or any other demand or criticism. We don't *have* to do anything. We are *choosing* to live with more love, peace and joy in our lives. In any moment, this is a choice. If we choose to see who we are in fear...so be it. We can just observe and know we are **choosing** that experience of fear. Still creating! Just creating what we don't want!

EXERCISE 5A

WHAT IS YOUR LANGUAGE OF FEAR?

1. Take this opportunity to write a brief list of how your inner voice of fear speaks to you.

Observe the Voice of Fear—Don't Judge It!

Spirit (a conduit for love), knows only how to be and give of itself, which of course is love. Acceptance of where you are in this very moment insures you are listening to the guidance and support of this inner voice of love. Acceptance does not mean you are not choosing to grow; it simply moves the ego out of the way to allow you to grow. As you hear yourself struggle with the Inner Voice of fear, one affirmation that I find works well for many people is the following:

*In this moment, I am choosing to be **even more** accepting of myself.*

By stating this affirmation, you not only demonstrate to yourself you are willing to take control of your life, you also send gratitude to the ego as it reminds you that you are in need of more love in some part of yourself. The very act of choosing to send your ego off with love insures your movement toward greater awakening to your Spirit. To be able to shine light on your ego (darkness) is the ultimate act of love. Love shines light in the darkness and therefore it is no longer capable of staying dark. Light always reigns over darkness. Go into a dark closet and shine the tiniest flashlight. It is impossible for the closet to remain in complete darkness.

The love within each of us is the light that empowers the healing of fear. You are that light. Without your discovery of the **unlimited power to create** that lies within each of us, we are dimmer en masse. **Please...Shine.**

Thoughts and Words Have Real Energy—

Power to Create

Remember that our words carry with them the power to create peace or chaos. In fact they are doing exactly that inside our head every moment of every day. Much of our negative stress comes simply from our internal dialogue. We create what we focus on.

At every moment your inner voices are communicating with you. Most of these messages will be hardly noticeable at all, until you pay close attention. The inner voice of fear, if not managed, leads us down a road that is based only on the past.

Language Can Create New Beginnings or Rehash Old Stories

I always think of the subconscious mind as a storage place for old stories of the past which in theory should allow our conscious mind to stay in the present. I did say, in theory.

The problem with this is that most of us, most of the time, are living in the past or the future, busily rehashing, re-creating, re-visiting and generally ensuring the past stays alive in the stories we relive, over and over and over again. In doing this we come to believe the past equals the future…and nothing could be further from the truth. The past is gone. It appears only to repeat itself because our thoughts are stuck in the stories of old. We become victims of our past experience until we choose to think, do, say and believe something different about the present.

The Inner Voice of Fear is a Learned Behavior that can be Replaced

The inner voice of fear is the voice that has picked up the discipline and the fearful training where our well meaning parents left off, in an effort to teach us "correct" behavior or what to "watch out for" to be safe. Most of what we have learned to be the truth about ourselves and the world around us is based on fear. But how could they have known any different?

Your voice of fear is the one that says in some way we are not good enough just as we are. It is the voice that says relationships are dangerous and life wasn't meant to be easy. It is the place that gives birth to every judgment that we have.

BECOME AWARE,
MANAGE THE UNCONSTRUCTIVE DIALOG

For most people, this voice of the past is chatting to us all day, every day. Becoming aware of it and creating new thoughts by choosing to live in the moment are the first two steps to managing our unconstructive inner dialog. As we do this, we create new pathways in the brain and new subconscious beliefs that empower not hinder the outcomes that we choose in our lives.

The External Voice of Fear

The messages from the subconscious that are passed on to the conscious become our external voices. These are the words we share as our thoughts and opinions; this is the personality that we form. Speaking engages our physiology and this physiology changes our body chemistry. As vocal chords vibrate, they affect our physical state. As we hear the words and feel the emotions that we attach to the word, we react.

As we continue to repeat any statement in our internal and external voices, we come to *know* it to be true... regardless of its validity.

List a few UNTRUTHS (self criticisms) courtesy of your voice of FEAR:

EXERCISE 5B

BECOME AWARE OF THE QUESTIONS YOU ASK YOURSELF AND OTHERS

Being a speaker and a person who adores the power of words, I am keenly aware of the choices I and others are making as we speak. I hear so many people asking the kind of questions that can only produce negative answers. Instead of asking, "How can I improve the way I feel?" they ask, "Why do I always feel so lousy?" Instead of asking, "What can I do to bring more joy into my life?" they ask, "Why is there so little joy in the world?"

If you ask a question that only has a negative answer, you will get exactly what you asked for!

Examples:

Why me? Why does everything turn to sour when I touch it?

What? Is your life so completely terrible? Oh and if you don't mind I'd be ever so grateful if you'd kindly keep your hands off me if this be the case. No offence but I do prefer my usual sweetness to the sour promise, thanks so much! What, you can't see it?

How come all the promotions at work pass me by?

Do they? All of them? You mean even the ones you really, really want and do all that it takes to get? All of them? Wow. Are you in the line of work that brings out your passion? I'm just wondering that's all…

Why are all the good guys married or gay?

Holy dooly! Every single one of them? And not one single one? I'm suddenly depressed. I was kind of hoping there was just one out there for me! Mind you, gay guys do make great guy pals…

By now you might be imagining that a private session with me can be somewhat unsatisfying if you were just looking to find pity in all your many perceived problems! While I feel compassion and great empathy for the part of an individual who has not yet learned they have real power, what is more important is proving to them otherwise. I have a keen ear for "the victim," having been an expert myself and having to find my way out, for the most part on my own. I have learned the importance of maintaining a disciplined approach to the dead end question.

1. Observe yourself and others. Pay particular attention to how you ask questions that can produce only a negative answer. See if you can catch yourself and or others asking a dead end question at least five times over the next few days.

Stay on this task until you have succeeded. It's not a matter of IF you are surrounded by dead end questions, it's a matter of how many you can identify! Watch the news, listen at work, at the grocery store, on public transport, you will find them.

EXERCISE 5C

BECOME AWARE OF THE STATEMENTS YOU MAKE

The same applies to statements that have nowhere to go but downward. If we make negative statements about ourselves and our world, we will confirm these things to be true in the way we respond to our beliefs. We will set out to prove ourselves to be correct—because none of us wants to be wrong. We might not do so consciously, but I have seen how easily I attract the perfect situations, people and circumstances to validate my belief systems.

Examples:

My life will always be like this because I'm shy

(And that can't be changed?)

I know Joe Blogs will get that promotion over me.

(Well, with that belief, you're certainly giving him the better chance!)

Observe yourself and others. Pay particular attention to the statements you make that can only produce a negative outcome. See if you can catch yourself making a dead end statement at least twice this week!

EXERCISE 5D

OPPORTUNITY TO PRACTICE GREATER AWARENESS OF YOUR INNER VOICES

What is your inner dialog saying about you and the world you live in? Is your language critical or affirming most of the time? Does it support your true-self or does it sabotage you?

1. I recently noticed my inner voice of fear popping in when:

   (Describe the story and your inner voice's response to the detail)

Is your voice of love challenging your voice of fear yet? It may take a little time to begin to notice this internal battle that goes on in our head. Just become more aware.

2. I recently noticed my inner voice of love challenging old beliefs when:

It is most likely you will discover that you both support and sabotage through the use of your language. To have a life filled with greater love and peace, our task is to increase our focus on that which serves us, and decrease our focus on that which does not. So why have we focused on our shadow or ego selves for most of this book so far? Good question!

Our ego is not *bad*—it merely presents an opportunity to know where we need more love or to simply feel safe.

P.S. When I or others pick up on my fearful behavior I simply say…

Be patient with me

I am a work in progress

I am just savoring the unveiling of such a masterpiece!

EXERCISE 5E

OPPORTUNITY TO PRACTICE AWARENESS OF YOUR LANGUAGE THROUGH CREATIVE WRITING

By now, if you have been taking up the opportunities to practice your own unique way of discovering who you are, you will notice the changes in your mood, feelings, ideas and activities.

You are not any of these things. *You* are the part that is able to observe these things. Notice how your pen flows when you commit to the exercises? Notice how it gets easier as you practice?

This activity should be practiced daily for a minimum of one week. You can play with this activity whenever you feel you are losing focus on who you really are and what is important to you.

This writing exercise is particularly powerful if you allow yourself to write continually, regardless of what you see forming on the page. Just let it happen.

1. **Observe your actions** and which voice you find yourself taking action from most often.

2. **Continue to write down** your observations over the next week.

   Write a list of what brings you joy. Ask yourself what brings you joy and without hesitation begin to write for a solid five minutes. Do not put your pen down and do not stop writing until your five minutes is up. Include abstract ideas. Example: One of the things on the list could be something as simple as the color blue. Don't judge. Any need for judgment is an act of resistance provided courtesy of your ego.

   Use the blank pages at the back of the book or your own writing journal. Head it up as follows:

a) **How I Act Out of Love and Fear**—Remember to date it.

b) **Joyful Continual Writing**—Date this one also. It's great to look back on later.

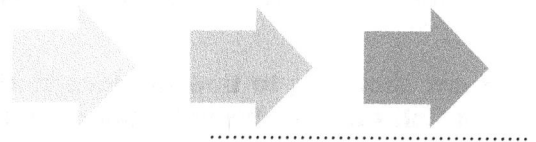

I give myself permission to observe myself and my world without judgment. As I do this, I acknowledge that my life is my own and I am not held back by the past.

All judgment can only be based on past experience, and I choose to live in this moment, embracing every opportunity to be all that I am

I am learning to trust that all is in perfect order in my life, because I am a part of the unflawed universal law

I am choosing to find the love that is within myself and all others who naturally support my awakening.

6. replacing fear with the ultimate power (love)

How are you going with that concept of letting go of judgment and replacing it with discernment?

What we are trying to do in this exercise is observe our egos; the judgmental, fearful part of ourselves. At the same time we are trying not to judge ourselves as we observe.

I recognize this is easier said than done. Almost all of our conditioning dictates that negative behavior, thoughts and/or feelings should be punished in some way. Here we suggest these "fearful" or ego parts of the self are only a need for more love. You are in the process of discovering more about the places inside you that are wounded or tender.

EXERCISE 6A

EGO OBSERVATION LIST—FINDING THE SORE SPOTS

Write a list of some of the ways you have noticed you feel, think or behave negatively. These are your ego observations. Remember there is no need to judge these, only be aware of them. True and sustainable change never comes from guilt.

These ego, or so-called "negative" observations are in reality only the part within us that doesn't know we are designed perfectly, as is the universe, to support every small detail of our life's journey. We want for nothing. **Everything we need is already a part of who we are; we just have yet to unveil or acknowledge it.** This part within our mini-me is fearful and it tries to run our lives, often (and unfortunately) quite successfully.

All the items on your list of negative observations are simply an opportunity for you to notice the parts within you that need to feel safe. They all stem from some form of conditioning that has told you that you are in some way not good enough, or you will not be protected, safe.

Hypothetical Example—Finding the Niggling Little Sore Spot

If for example someone were to write on their ego observation list, "I *get* angry when things don't go my way," they might be demonstrating a desire to control their environment in order to feel safe. Their behaviors may be such things as these:

- Controlling

- Temperamental

- Selfish

- Angry

In fact, rather than what we might easily judge this person to be; a nasty, angry adult who is selfish and controlling, the truth behind the behavior is far more likely to be that in this particular situation (not always), a part of him is a frightened child who has an unmet need to feel safe. It is quite likely his fear would be that if he did not control his environment, something frightening or at least unpleasant would happen. This idea could have been formed from the seemingly most insignificant occurrence when he was a small child, or it could be from a lifetime of abuse. The actual "story" is unimportant at this stage. What is extremely relevant is the fear itself.

Our ability to identify the fears that make up our wounds is important to insure we can more easily embrace our dark or ego side, removing its power over us. As we do so, we eradicate darkness with light, and we replace fear with love. We can then move from self-judgment and into real healing.

Wounds of the past don't always present themselves in the form of obvious fears such as shyness, anxiousness or debilitating phobias. They can look aggressive, defensive and spiteful, sometimes even strong in their ability to fend off the people and situations that will cause them to revert to their child-like fears. Don't be fooled. Anything but unconditional love is fear. Rather than hate those parts of yourself, love them. Nothing else but your own love can or ever will have the genuine power to eliminate fear from your life.

The very choice to ***observe without judgment*** is an act of self-love in itself. Gradually, as we continue to do this, we become less and less afraid to be honest with ourselves and with others, allowing ourselves freedom to be all that we are.

It really does get easier as you practice.

YOU are where you are and you are choosing to make some loving changes.

Pat yourself on the back as you do so.

If you're negative with yourself it will only take longer.

And remember you are not alone.

The best part of this practice is as you become more able to view yourself without criticism; you become more loving not only of yourself, but also of others. You will find that as you allow yourself to be all of the many colors and shades of your true-self, you are more able to be patient with others as they unfold and discover their own uniqueness.

EXERCISE 6B

FINDING AND NURTURING THE SORE SPOTS

1.　Take your ego observations list in **Exercise 6a** and try to identify what the fear might be behind each of them.

EGO OBSERVATION

....

Example:
Anger when things don't go my way

....

MY FEAR IS

....

If I don't control my world it might control me!

....

Nurturing the Sore Spots

Imagine yourself as the two parts of yourself, the adult and the child.

Now that you have your list of specific fears, acknowledge that this child is in need of your love not your criticism in order to feel safe. Remember these parts of you are not bad—they are quite simply your wounds of conditioning, created at some point in your life. Each time we come into a situation that stirs fear, the wound is reopened and there is only one person who can truly close it forever—that would be **you.** Others can nurture, support and feel compassion toward you; however, nothing but the love of yourself (demonstrated by the choice to do something different) can heal any wound forever and create new beliefs.

As we learn and then choose to understand our ego self is simply the part that is fearful and in need of love, we can more easily release the fear and find greater joy and freedom.

As You Practice Please Remember...

`If a small child were fearful in a world that felt out of his/ her control, would you try to comfort him or her? Or would you reprimand the child, sending them into a dark corner and ignoring their need for love?`

Why then, as we approach our own darkness as adults, should we make it difficult? There is no need for judgment, name calling ("I'm so stupid for feeling like this"), or any other form of self abuse. Your fears are the same as the fears of a small child. In fact, the part of you that is fearful is the child within you.

2. Now that you have discovered some of the fears behind your behavior, practice being as kind to yourself today as you would be to a wounded child.

    How might you choose to do that?

EXERCISE 6C

FINDING LOVE—NATURALLY

1. Write some notes on times when you are giving of yourself and it feels effortless. This might be when you are around children or doing your art. Note where you naturally feel love, loved and loving.

2. Note some times recently when you chose to feel empowered instead of fearful, a time when previously you might have chosen otherwise. You might have chosen to take care of yourself in some way instead of playing a victim or a martyr. You may have chosen to find the love in another person instead of disliking them. Find the ways your efforts to learn more about true love has made you feel good about yourself.

    I chose love over fear when:

Let no one ever come to you
without them leaving
better and happier

– Mother Teresa

7. clarity comes from the inside… you will find it if only you look!

A Week in Clear View

As you continue to write down your thoughts and experiences, you clear the clutter in your head to make room for your inner wisdom to be heard. Write as much and as often as you can. Release the busyness in your mind as often as possible. If you need more space, remember you can always buy or create your own journal.

EXERCISE 7A

CLARITY EXERCISE DAY 1:
OPPORTUNITY TO GAIN GREATER CLARITY THROUGH WRITING

Write about anything at all. Simply download any busyness in your head and leave room for your true-self to guide the ship. Use the back of the book for more space or add to your own writing journal.

Hey Journal,
I just wanted to clear my head so I'm going to share a few things here…

EXERCISE 7B

CLARITY THROUGH MEDITATION

Five minutes of meditation can change your day. To get to the place of mental stillness, put on some relaxation music, a guided relaxation or the *Permission to Let Go* CD track 2 breathing exercises. Don't let your ego mind tell you your meditation won't make a difference. It is the greatest tool we have to support the unveiling of our natural clarity. By the way, just because this exercise only takes up a few lines in the book and seconds to read doesn't mean it's time to go onto the next activity without doing this one!

EXERCISE 7C

CLARITY EXERCISE DAY 2: CLARITY THROUGH FEELING GRATITUDE

I have discovered the universe works in cooperation with gratitude. In fact, being grateful before I can actually see any outcomes or results implies I trust that all is in perfect order. I know each of my greatest visions of my grandest life are being met before my eyes. And I am grateful for the process of experiencing myself through the lives and situations surrounding me. I have learned to be grateful for whatever is presented to me in life, because I'm always being presented with exactly what I created with my thoughts and therefore, exactly what I chose in order to re-discover the truth about all that I am.

1.   Try to find at least 5 things that you're grateful for. If that's too is easy, go for more! **I feel grateful for...**

EXERCISE 7D

CLARITY EXERCISE DAY 3: GAINING GREATER AWARENESS

1. Since you began working in this book you are likely to have noticed you are becoming more conscious of the way you think, the way you feel and the way you behave. Writing about this increased awareness supports greater clarity about what you want, how you feel, what else you might need to do, and so on. Before you commence writing, allow yourself two minutes to close your eyes and breathe.

    *   Breathe in focus, clarity, an open heart and mind.

    *   Breathe out any blockages that limit your highest truth and your willingness to be unlimited in your clarity.

2. Note how you feel after a time of focus and stillness. Words such as good and fine are not allowed. (Major cop-out!) Be specific about how you feel for example, tired, happy, excited, sad, energized, hopeless, and so on.

3. The seemingly smallest observations are important in order that you honor your efforts. Remember the only joy you can experience is in this moment. It's all about the journey not the destination.

    *   *I am becoming more aware of some of the ways I'm changing*

4. Describe any changed behavior in others, outcomes and responses to your choice to live more consciously.

    *   *My changes affect my relationships in ways that feel comfortable and uncomfortable to me.*

"IN THIS MOMENT, I AM CHOOSING TO BE LESS JUDGMENTAL ON MYSELF."

EXERCISE 7E

CLARITY EXERCISE DAY 4: WRITING ABOUT EGO TO GAIN GREATER CLARITY

1. Writing about our ego exposes it! It also helps us become observers rather than judge and jury as we read back with interest and hopefully amusement on how this thing called our ego actually thinks it's going to get away ruling the roost much longer. How is your ego trying to play games with you lately? In what areas of your life would you say you can be critical or judgmental?

    Sometimes I can be tough on myself and on others by…

2. List some ways in which your ego has been trying to limit you. For more ideas on how the ego comes out to play, refer to the second step in the Dance of Opportunity called "Check Your Intentions" under the sub-headings:

    • *In love*   • *In fear*   *Check out the Love and Fear in Action table in the Dance of Opportunity.*

    I am becoming more aware of the way my ego tries to limit my freedom and my joy.
    (Example: Ego tells you you're not getting anywhere by becoming more aware of who you are.)

3. How have you noticed you are currently changing old limiting patterns? This question relates to how you practice rather than what outcomes you have manifested from these efforts.

    Some of the ways I'm currently changing old limiting patterns are…

4. Permission is really about allowing ourselves to fully appreciate the gift of being in the game rather than needing to win it all the time. Having said that, we all like to enjoy the successes. So how are you noticing your efforts paying off? What is changing in your life because of your choice to further connect to your true and more empowered self?

5. Do not leave this one blank!

    I feel pretty good about myself because:

I am learning that true love starts with being gentle on myself as I grow and discover the truth about who I am.

EXERCISE 7F

CLARITY EXERCISE DAY 5: CLARITY THROUGH NOTICING YOUR POWER

I know I am not a victim to my past and I prove this to myself every day.

Some of the ways I demonstrate my authentic power are:

EXERCISE 7G

CLARITY EXERCISE DAY 6:
THE GRADUAL PROCESS OF AWAKENING AND LETTING GO OF PAST STORIES

Sometimes I find it difficult to be patient with myself or others. I allow myself understanding and continue to move forward.

I've noticed that lately that I'm becoming more aware of:

My new awareness is helping me be more loving to myself by way of:

EXERCISE 7H

CLARITY EXERCISE DAY 7:
CLARITY THROUGH NOTICING MOMENTS OF LOVE IN MY LIFE

I feel more aware of love in my world and within myself in the following ways:

1.

2.

3.

4.

5.

6.

7.

Remember to breathe in love and clarity. Breathe out any blockages that might limit you from opening up to being present in love, here and now.

Track 2 on the *Permission to Let Go* CD can help you work on breathing techniques.

a life without love

is merely existing in a cold illusion

8. you're not "normal" —you're unique!

The words "normal" and "family" were never meant to be used in the same sentence!

You might have what you consider to be a *normal* family. You might not. What is important here is not so much whether you do, but what your definition of normal is, and then how you relate to that definition.

If I had a dollar for every time a client said to me, "I don't come from a normal family," I would probably be writing this book from a lavish hotel suite on a secluded island, arriving in my personal jet accompanied by all of my closest friends and favorite family members (just the normal ones of course).

There are many reasons for us to look at this concept of normality, but for the most part it is important we begin to see how this idealistic notion of *normal* is the basis or foundation of our core conditioning and therefore part of what we base our identity upon. Unfortunately, because it is more of an unattainable and abstract notion rather than a tangible reality, we are left in our striving for it, and feeling at some level unsuccessful.

It is also important to remove the myth that others are in some way more, or less, or better off or worse off or have a greater or lesser chance of happiness than you do.

Together we will observe the idealistic concept of normality versus the truth about our uniqueness so you can let go of others' expectations of who you should be and embrace more fully who you *really* are. Interestingly, I have observed with myself and with many others that we will always be of greater service to ourselves, others and the world around us when being our true selves—even if it is sometimes hard to see.

Who Sold Us "Normal" in the First Place?

When you take the time to observe this "normal phenomenon," it can become almost humorous. We are being sold comparative thinking almost everywhere we look and in most of what we hear. Normality in one form or another is being sold to us in every advertisement we see and it does so by pointing out our "flaws" or our "abnormality."

They tell us that men must have smooth faces or very finely groomed beards—so thanks to the providers of razors you can buy a magic image saver that will insure you don't have to walk around looking like a caveman, (translation: abnormal). Women must have smooth legs and heaven forbid if the armpits get hairy—so thanks to the provider of the more feminine blade, you can also buy the woman's version of the same razor because we couldn't be seen with the black shaver denoting the masculine influence! Pink is so much more feminine, and all women must be feminine. It's normal! Well, that is of course unless we are European women and then in some places naked legs are considered disgusting. There too we must conform to normality or find the courage to stand out from the normal crowd.

Normal people have a close relationship with everyone in their family and they call home regularly (or they feel guilty about not doing so). Just look at the telephone companies' advertising campaigns. They use the long distance family to demonstrate how wonderful we will all feel when we call home and make Grandma's day. It gets you right in the heart doesn't it?

We have been, and continue to be sold, this idea of normality in so many ways in our day-to-day lives. Remember the "*Waltons?*" "*Leave it to Beaver?*" "*Happy Days?*" (Oh dear, am I older than you? In that case think the opposite to the "*Simpsons*" and "*Family Guy*"). I remember looking at those television families when I was a child and sometimes literally crying for what I didn't have. Now I know I wasn't the only one crying! It was supposed to be the norm to have a happy mommy and daddy always looking out for their children before contemplating any need they might have themselves! Siblings politely tease one another at worst and every night the whole family should gently call out from their beds, "G'nite Ma." And it would always lovingly be met with a warm, "G'nite John Boy." That's normal in your family right?

Apparently now it is also normal to be completely cellulite and wrinkle free, sporting a six-pack washboard stomach regardless of our age; and it is absolutely natural to have a desperate, constant hunger for sex. You only have to refer to music videos, billboards and magazines if you want the latest scoop on just how hungry, overtly sexy, svelte and youthful you should remain in order to fit into what our current society is deeming to be normal.

Apparently it is also normal to hate those who are different from us, to kill and torture "in the name of God and country," to misuse power and to lie in the name of politics or media. Regardless of whether we agree with the rightness or wrongness of these acts, we are coming to accept them as part of our day-to-day lives in the society in which we live. While I like to believe most of us wouldn't actually commit these acts ourselves, we are gradually becoming less and less surprised as we witness it daily on our televisions. Subtly the hate, the killing and lies spread, because without a conscious choice to do otherwise, we are being conditioned through repetition to believe it is normal.

"All that is necessary for evil to succeed is for good men to do nothing"

– Edmund Burre

We can all argue that intellectually we have the common sense to know otherwise, yet desensitization through repeatedly seeing and experiencing the same things over and over inevitably has an effect on how we think, feel and behave—consciously or subconsciously.

On the other hand, feelings such as abundance, happiness, peace and joy cannot be based on what is normal by anyone else's standards. They are unique to each one of us and I suspect this in itself contributes partly to why so few people know how to attain them. Being unique is not being sold! We cannot be controlled by our external environment when our guidance comes from within (our true-self) rather than from false information and temporary fads.

It seems to me societies since the beginning of time have been trying to recapture this intuitive knowing that we are all connected and part of one bigger picture. The difficulty is that rather than discovering how our unique offerings all fit together to create collective greatness, we have boxed, packaged and limited ourselves by trying to be the same, to fit in and of course to be normal. Being *connected as one* and *being the same as,* are two very different things.

External or societal beliefs tend to change with time. They do not necessarily create happiness, and yet we are sold the idea they will do so from the moment we are born. These things we seek as we reach out toward others are only found within ourselves. Only I can be responsible for deciding what will bring me the greatest joy in my own life and only I know what feels normal to me.

When I ask many people what they really want in their heart of hearts, I am always amazed at how few have any idea at all. I ask them then, how could anybody else know what will bring us joy, if we don't?

Normal is the easy way out. It is a part of our victim selves in action. In place of having to know ourselves, we can let others dictate who we should be and hope there is a grain of joy in there somewhere but if not, poor me! And this is what we call normal. I don't know about you but that just doesn't do it for me!

Reality check

You are not normal

you are **unique**

and thank God for that!

A Unique Week

This week we're going to observe consciously what the "normal world" has decided will bring us happiness. Wealth, beauty, status, fashion— they're all great, and certainly what we're being sold every day as a means to happiness. If you buy the product, you will gain pleasure or rid yourself of pain. You will not only be normal, you will be everything you've ever wanted to be and more! True? Unlikely.

We all have something unique to offer and our task here is to discover what that really is, not necessarily what the outside world believes it is, but rather what you know from the inside to be true about who you are. Take some time to listen to your own wisdom.

Incoming Information—In the Name of Norm

Over the next week begin to pay particularly close attention to how advertising plays with your emotions and your beliefs about who you are, what is "normal," what you "should" look like, how shiny you hair should be, how you should smell—all in the name of the norm.

The basis of advertising is to stir emotion. You are surrounded by this message of normality every day, be it true or false. Check in and see what emotions they are stirring. I don't suggest they will all be negative. In fact the goal is to make you feel good as you imagine having their product. How do you feel if you knew you could not have their product or the image attached to it? It's worth a thought.

The average women's clothing size in Australia is size 14. Is that what the advertising industry says is normal? I think not.

I asked 15 teenage girls what they thought the average Australian size was:

- 10 out of 15 thought it was size 8 (size 1-2 in America)

- 4 thought it was size 10

- 1 thought it was size 12

They all reported feeling a lot better when they knew the real statistic.

In America the average weight for white Caucasian women aged 20-29 is 131 lb. (59.8 kg).

The average weight for an African American woman the same age is 150 lb. (68 kg).

If I had guessed the average weight of women in America based on the magazines and television shows (which is what we see in Australia), I would have said it was somewhere around 105–115 lb. (48-52 kg). What do you think? It is also interesting to note the difference in weight based on racial heritage. This difference can demonstrate many things, from how various races carry greater or lesser amounts of muscle mass, to differences in digestive systems. I don't claim to understand the many intricacies of analyzing this information, nor do we need to for the purpose of the exercise. I simply provide these statistics to demonstrate we are all different and these differences are not necessarily modeled or respected when we are being told what size clothes we should be wearing in order to be "attractive" or "normal."

If we were to take the average music video clip and assume from that the normal weight for women aged 20-30, I suggest that the average woman as seen in the true statistics would suddenly feel quite overweight—as so many do.

If we are to make the road to self-acceptance a little easier,

let's start by dealing with the facts

rather than trying to live up to the illusions

that we are being sold as normality.

[2] From www.halls.md/on/women-weight-b.htm, Hall's Weight Chart, Steven B. Halls, MD, FRCPC and John Hanson, MSc.

EXERCISE 8A

OPPORTUNITY TO PRACTICE DAY 1: ILLUSION VERSUS NORMALITY

1.   Record: Each day for seven days, record your feelings about the messages you receive from work, friends, family, television, and so forth that state what is supposed to be normal.

2.   Now that you are intentionally becoming aware of the illusion, talk to others about your discoveries. You might be a great support to someone who is struggling to meet the unrealistic expectations of our society.

EXERCISE 8B

OPPORTUNITY TO PRACTICE DAY 2: CHALLENGE BY INTERVIEW

1.   **The interview challenge:** Challenge your idea of normal by finding out other people's ideas. As a study project, interview a minimum of three people outside your family and immediate friendship group (and more if you want more accurate statistics), and ask them questions that challenge your beliefs. For example, if you feel less than part of the norm because you become self-conscious when you walk into certain rooms, ask a question such as, "Do you ever feel self-conscious when you walk into a room?"

This is something you can use any time you need a reminder about the gift of uniqueness. The more people you interview or share this concept with, the surer you will become convinced everyone has their own little quirks, interesting mannerisms and idiosyncrasies. Nobody is exactly like anyone else, and yet you might be surprised as you discover everyone is also very much the same. We all want to be loved for who we are. We all want Permission to be all that we are.

2.   My observations today relating to my perception of normality are:

EXERCISE 8C

OPPORTUNITY TO PRACTICE DAY 3: A UNIQUE OBSERVATION

1. Continue to observe your feelings around the messages you receive.

    What should a normal person of your age be wearing these days? What should a normal family behave like, according to the subtle messages in our multi-faceted world? What is a normal behavior at work? What is an abnormal behavior? How white should your teeth be? What clothing size should you be? What about hair under your armpits ladies? Disgusting or accepted? According to what country? Guys, can you be successful without driving a nice car? Just enjoy being the observer. Record your observations.

EXERCISE 8D

OPPORTUNITY TO PRACTICE DAY 4: HOW ARE YOU JUDGING YOUR OWN UNIQUENESS?

1. How do I judge normality? How have I bought into believing that there is a certain standard everyone must meet to be normal?

2. How do I feel I fit into the word normal compared with the rest of my family?

3. How/when/in what areas of my life do I judge myself as less than others?

4. How/when/in what areas of my life do I judge myself as better than others?

5. What do I believe I gain from these judgments? Dig deep. You will always have an investment that either relieves you of fear/pain or provides you with pleasure/love.

For example your judgments might help you believe you are helpless so you don't have to change. They might make you feel better than others in one way or another which helps compensate for where you feel less than them. Discover your own investment in judgment.

EXERCISE 8E

OPPORTUNITY TO PRACTICE DAY 5: FOCUS ON UNIQUENESS

1. **Morning** (Five-minute focus session)

    Take the following idea with you throughout the day. Really try to remember to pay attention to people's uniqueness, regardless of whether you like it or you find it difficult. Just observe. **Repeat the following affirmation five times before you start your day:**

    Today I choose to learn more about the value of each unique offering provided by the many people who touch my life in large and small ways.

2.   **Lunch** (Two-minute focus session)

Repeat the above affirmation five times in the middle of your day.
Remember the importance of breathing fully and using the breath to focus on your affirmation.
Using your breath as you say the affirmation:

Breathe in—Release and say: **Today I choose to learn more**

Breathe in—Release and say: **about the value of each unique offering**

Breathe in—Release and say: **provided by the many people who touch my life**

Breathe in—Release and say: **in large and small ways.**

Repeat four more times.

3.   **Evening** (Minimum of 10 minutes of writing)

Record some of the ways in which people touched your life today. If you feel there was nobody who touched your life in any way, you must not have come into contact with anyone, via telephone, television, radio, or otherwise. If you did have contact with people and still cannot find one way in which they touched your life to make a difference, you're not looking! Keep trying and fill in this exercise on a day that you are able. Whatever you do, don't leave it blank! This exercise is important to your overall process. Enjoy.

EXERCISE 8F

OPPORTUNITY TO PRACTICE DAY 6: AFFIRMING THE TRUTH

1. **Morning** (Five- minute focus session)

   Take the following idea with you throughout the day. Really try to remember to pay attention to your own uniqueness, regardless of whether you like it or you find it difficult. Just observe.
   Repeat the following affirmation five times before you start your day:

   ### As I recognize the unique offerings of others, I also allow my own uniqueness to be made more visible. I am one of a kind and I value the qualities that make me...Me!

2. **Lunch** (Two- minute focus session)

   Repeat the above affirmation five times in the middle of your day and briefly record how you feel immediately following the practice of positive affirmation.

3. **Evening** (Minimum of 5 minutes of continual writing)

Using the blank pages in the spare note pages at the back of the book, or in your own journal, allow yourself to write continually for five minutes. Do not let your pen stop moving. It doesn't matter what goes on the page as long as your intention is to stay on the topic below:

- **Some of the qualities I like the most in myself are:**

CONGRATULATIONS...

Look at who you are!

As you continue to discover

your own uniqueness, we all benefit

thanks for making the effort!

EXERCISE 8G

UNIQUE OPPORTUNITY DAY 7: HONOR YOUR UNIQUENESS

Recently I went out and bought myself three new hats. I have always loved the look of hats, but more importantly they highlight the part of myself that is quite playful. As I write these words I am wearing a great old English style men's peak hat that has a cute little button that flips up the corner of the cap. I feel like me!

This book has only found its words as I stay true to who I am at my core. I have not been able to write on those days when I've had too much going on in my own head. I have been forced to take care of my own unique journey or the words simply stopped.

That is true of anyone's life. If you are blocked by the things that limit you, your dreams and visions will have a great deal of difficulty becoming your reality unless you honor your own unique journey. Part of that nurturing is paying attention to what makes you feel most like you.

1. Over the next two days focus on acknowledging the things that make you feel alive.

    Think of things that are a part of who you are, regardless of whether they are a part of who others might think you are. Become more aware of these things. Ask friends if they think you have any little quirky ways. List some things that make you feel like you.

2. You may not feel like buying new hats, but I challenge you to do at least two things each day over the next two days. Record how you feel and what you observe.

Day 1

1.

2.

Day 2

1.

2.

may your unique offerings bring as much joy to you as it does to the universe.

2. To honor my own uniqueness, each day this week I will do at least one thing from the list below:

WHAT I WILL DO	BY THIS DATE
....	....
....	....
....	....
....	....
....	....
....	....
....	....
....	....
....	....
....	....
....	....
....	....

you are a unique part of this universal puzzle
no less than the moon and the stars
as you shine your brilliant light that radiates from within
you offer up the most perfect gifts
that only you can offer!

....

EXERCISE 8H

OPPORTUNITY TO FIND THE CENTER OF PEACE, LOVE AND WISDOM

This is a good opportunity to listen to the "Candle Meditation" on track 4 if you have the *Permission to Let Go* CD. If not, you could do the guided visualization below together with a friend. If neither is an option today, read the meditation below and then take yourself on a journey to wherever it leads you. Enjoy the process.

The Candle Meditation

The Candle Meditation is a very gentle and beautiful way in which to find your center of peace. If you have someone who might also enjoy sharing this experience, you may choose to take turns giving and receiving this guided journey into your spirit by reading it for one another. If you do this, it is important for the reader to give the other person time to take in each sentence. Don't rush and try to speak as gently as possible.

Once you've found someone to read for you just once, they usually want to do it again! I have found I get just as much from guiding others into connection with their spirit as I gain from being in my own meditations. Whether you are the reader or the traveler, both are a blessing.

Setting the Scene

✓ *Light at least one candle in the room and several if you choose. It is important you have at least one flame in clear view.*

✓ *Find your comfortable place of rest—where you can be alone for at least 10-20 minutes.*

✓ *Put one candle in a prominent position in front of you and if you like, turn on some relaxation music.*

Begin

✓ Stare into the flame. Watch it dance and sway and stand up tall and then become a small flame. Focus only on the flame.

✓ Imagine the center of the flame represents your spirit. Pure, alive, brilliant, gentle, dancing. All knowing.

✓ Continue to gaze into the flame for at least 20 breaths.

✓ **Breathe in** the warmth and the brilliance into your lungs. Imagine it moving through your veins and illuminating every cell in your body.

✓ **Breathe out** any darkness or fear that could limit you for experiencing the fullness of the light... the peacefulness of the experience and the freedom of simply being in this moment.

When you're ready, close your eyes. You will most likely continue to see the flame or a shadow of the flame for a period of time. Imagine the image that you see, the afterglow, is in fact the part of you that is the pure loving spirit within.

Take a few deep breaths. As you breathe in, think about the pure loving energy filling your body, your mind and your spirit. When you hold the air in, think about allowing that energy to filter through your body. When you release the air, imagine you are again releasing anything left that could limit the fullness of this experience. All of the negative toxins, thoughts and situations, are now leaving you forever.

Now drift. Allow the scent of the candles, the soft music, and the warmth of the room to fill your senses. Relax your head, your neck and shoulders. Pure love energy now flows through your body. Picture yourself surrounded by a white light. This is the protective light of pure love. It surrounds you and is flowing within you.

Go wherever you want to go. Continue to enjoy the spirit that you see. Imagine this to be your inner wisdom. Stare at it and enjoy. Sometimes it changes color. It might move around. Just take pleasure in being present with it. It is a reminder of the pure love that burns inside of you.

Allow yourself to go somewhere that makes you feel beautiful, lovable and worthy of all gifts.

Thoughts may come into your head. It's hard for them not to, especially at first. Allow them to come in, allow them to leave without judgment or ridicule. The aim is to give your brain a rest, while allowing your spirit to guide you. If you find the thoughts, rather than light and peace, are taking over your mind, open your eyes, stare at the candle again for a minute or so. Then close your eyes so that the flame appears again. Once again your inner wisdom is visible.

Take 10 deep breaths and release…all the while focusing on this place within you that burns in pure and unconditional love.

When you feel ready to return, and not before, gently wiggle your toes, move your shoulders, your legs, your hands and touch the ground with your feet. Feel the ground. At this point I say,

"I am grounded in my own truth and guided by my inner voice of wisdom. To all that is love, I thank you."

Open your eyes slowly when you're ready.

Sit quietly for a few minutes before doing anything if possible.

Whatever you focus on will feel real, regardless of its validity.

As you focus on the grandest desires of your spirit, **so shall you create!**

9. creating the changes you really desire

EXERCISE 9A

WHAT YOU FOCUS ON BECOMES YOUR REALITY

1. NEGATIVE FOCUS

*Write a few lines about a recent experience that felt **"negative"**. Sadness, anger, frustration, hate might be some of the emotions attached to such an event.*

Close your eyes. Sit with this memory. Focus on it for at least one minute. Feel it. Intensify the negative feelings.

How do you feel?

What is your body doing? Is there any tension in your face, neck, your hands, and your jaw? Start at the top of your head and gradually check-in with every part of your body until you get to your feet. Write down how your body is feeling and be as specific as you can.

Write a few lines about what your body is doing and how you feel after focusing on this negative event.

2.   THE FUNNEL

When you have written all that you want to write about this negative emotion, imagine a huge funnel like a large version of the ones you pour your petrol into when you've run out (not that I would know of course). See yourself pouring your used feelings into this magical funnel and allow it to take away any residue of negativity, sadness or pain from your mind and your body. Choose to let it go.

3. POSITIVE FOCUS

Write a few lines about a recent moment that felt very positive to you. Joy, peace, love, and/or happiness might be some of the emotions connected to such an experience.

Close your eyes. Sit with this happy memory for at least one minute. Feel it. Intensify the positive feelings.

How do you feel after focusing on these feelings?

What is your body doing now?

Is there any tension in your face, neck, your hands, your jaw or are you feeling more relaxed? Start at the top of your head and gradually check in with every part of your body until you get to your feet.

Write down how your body is feeling and be as specific as you can be.

What we focus on = our perceived reality

What are you making **real** in your life?

4. TRUE-SELF FOCUS

See yourself as having the things you choose in your life. Feel the gratitude of your state of life. As we do this, we ask our brain to work for us rather than letting it control us.

As I focus on my true-self

I quite naturally intensify the desire

that fuels me forward

toward my heart's great yearning to experience myself

in great joy and love

I believe we do our greatest soul work when we are living in accordance with our true desires, rather than living in a constant state of discipline. I learned this because my nickname used to be, *the rebel without a clue!* If you tell me I must go to the gym, I won't. If you tell me I should go to the gym, I might consider it but chances are I will quit in a month. If you tell me I could do it if I want to, I become empowered with choice. I have learned to focus on what my highest self truly desires, and what I focus on grows. I don't ask for the discipline to maintain a healthy life-style, I ask for the desire and focus on the wonderful feelings surrounding my good health.

As we focus on the desires of our true selves, we intensify the power we have to create our highest outcomes. What we will create is that which we truly desire, not that which the world around us dictates we should be, should have, should think, should feel or should do.

EXERCISE 9B

TRUE-SELF FOCUS (MORNING EXERCISE)

Before you answer the question below, remember to breathe-in clarity in whatever way you personally visualize that and breathe out any blockages that might limit the gift of this opportunity.

What do you want to focus on today that may support your journey toward even more happiness in your life?

What do you want to create today?

Once you have recorded your true desires today, take a deep breath. Open your mind and your heart to trusting it will be done. Be kind to yourself throughout this day and remember to continue to acknowledge your successes—even ones as seemingly small as noticing how your ego tried to play today. Each time you do this, you increase your awareness and gain power through choice.

TRUE-SELF FOCUS (EVENING EXERCISE)

Remember to breathe in peace and breathe out fear as you ask yourself today's questions.

Write a short (or long) note about how your focus affected your day:

Was there any time you noticed your ego trying to distract your focus from love to fear?

YES / NO

If not, be aware again tomorrow…and then the next day…until the answer is YES.

If so, how did it try to sabotage your day of creating the desires of your true-self?

How did you counteract your ego's attempt? If you didn't, try again tomorrow…and again the next day…and the next until you can answer this question.

congratulations
on completing these exercises

You are demonstrating commitment
to having **unlimited power**
over your own

thoughts' feelings and actions

MAKING SUSTAINABLE POSITIVE CHANGE

Opportunity To Simply Relax And Read!

Have you ever noticed that the idea of making some positive changes tends to appear far more attractive than the effort it takes to achieve the desired results?

I know too intimately the pain and frustration of having read so many inspirational self-help books and considered myself to be an intelligent human being who *gets it*, but was somehow not able to apply it! I had come to believe I had a serious piece missing in the puzzle.

More often than not, I am now able to sustain any change that I choose, and I have been able to teach many others to do the same. I no longer fear starting something just in case I quit when the going gets tough (or too good). Does any of this sound familiar to you? If not, congratulations, you already give yourself Permission to Dance in self-acceptance, responsibility and empowerment. If this does sound all too familiar, you're about to get some information that could change your life, forever. I know it changed mine.

The Only 3 Changes We Desire

I have discovered when people want to make a change in their lives; they really want to change three basic things. We make these changes by observing the need to change, accepting where we are now and where we want to be, then taking responsibility for both of these things, and choosing to move forward.

Regardless of the form a desired change comes in, I was able to identify that the core of every adjustment I was facilitating related to the same three things:

> *1. How we **think** about a certain thing*
>
> *2. How we **feel** about it*
>
> *3. How we **behave** in relation to it*

It may seem that we all want things from the material world—more money, a better job, better friends, more green lights when we're running late or an array of things that are found in our external world. However, I have learned through many years of self examination (being one of those rare and sometimes complex individuals who can't seem to muster up an ounce of motivation when money is the only carrot being dangled), I am still no different to those seeking the best car and the best house on the block. I still want to feel successful in my life. But what makes one person feel successful might not represent success to another.

My work in dealing with suicide really taught me a wonderful lesson about what sustains life and motivates us to move—and that is how we *feel* in relation to what is around us.

I further learned that how we feel is based on how we *think* about a particular thing and how we think and feel will determine how we will *behave*. I thought I had the formula. Then I realized these three things can be a bit like the chicken and the egg. Which comes first? That part of the equation seems to be unique to the individual, and even more so, depending on the situation that individual is relating to at a given time.

CASE STUDY[1]

I had a client Jill, who was struggling to coexist in the same house with her teenage daughter. (Welcome to the world of parenting teenagers!) She brought Andrea to me in the hope I could 'fix' this uncooperative, selfish and thoughtless teenager (all her adjectives, not mine). I found Andrea to be a charming, intelligent and a highly cooperative young woman. In fact, I quickly discovered that Andrea, highly receptive to the concepts I was working through with her and her mother, actually applied them immediately! Most teenagers repel any form of being controlled—perceived or otherwise. It's natural. (Not easy for us mere mortal parents, but certainly natural.) It's their time to learn the skills surrounding discernment, self exploration, how to think for themselves, exploring the world through their own eyes so they can make their own decisions about what feels right and wrong, true and false to them. Andrea learned quickly that by taking responsibility for her own thoughts, feelings and actions, she was more able to control the outcomes she actually wanted rather than feeling stuck and out of control of her world, as so many teenagers feel as they transmute from child to adult. She was hooked and she was moving forward quickly.

Jill on the other hand had many more years of negative conditioning. She was raised to believe you can't help how you feel and you can't help what you think, the greatest myth that allows others to control us. In fact, if you don't control what you think, you have thousands of messages through the mass media every day to confirm that limiting belief. Advertising agencies and governments alike absolutely thrive on the fact that most people are victims to their own thoughts.

EXERCISE 9C

AWARENESS OF FEARFUL CONDITIONING

Pay particular attention to the media and politicians and see if you can identify any way in which they may subtly and some not so subtly use fear to create need and/or dependence on their products and/or policies. It can be quite amusing when you look at the world from this perspective—more humorous of course once you get past the feelings that surround manipulation, deception and dishonesty.

Out of Control

Jill continued to struggle with looking at her own contribution to Andrea's behavior. Her paradigm was based on her own upbringing, which commanded fear. Do it or else! Back in those days, we didn't wait around to find out, or else what? Things are different now.

Gradually Jill learned that taking responsibility for her thinking, her feelings and her behavior had nothing to do with blame or regret—and everything to do with having the power to create the kind of relationship she wanted to have with her daughter.

All names have been changed in respect of client privacy and protection.

I do not mean to imply all members of the media and all politicians are manipulative, deceptive and /or dishonest. I have worked in the media and I know firsthand there are some remarkable people who have gone into these professions to make a difference and they manage to maintain great integrity under challenging circumstances. For each of these people I am grateful. We need more of you.

The most important thing Jill learned to do was to take responsibility for every interaction she experienced with Andrea. When her daughter left her room a mess, Jill historically had a thought pattern that went something like this: "My daughter is a lazy, thoughtless person who is not going to have a clue how to run a household." Which actually translates to: "I have done a lousy job of preparing my daughter for the adult world and I feel bad and somewhat afraid about that!"

This thinking created a series of feelings. Jill was able to identify these feelings as the following:

- I feel bad about my own shortcomings as a mother

- I feel afraid she is ill-prepared for adulthood and that's my fault

- I feel angry at myself for the way I handle the situation

- I feel angry at Andrea for disregarding me and how I want my house to be kept

- I feel frustrated that I don't know what to do

- I feel hurt that Andrea has no respect for me as a mother

All of these feelings were based on her thinking or her beliefs about a particular thing. It will be no surprise then that her behavior will then be based on how she feels.

Jill acted out her painful feelings in destructive ways, with such responses as mother/daughter yelling matches, pillow punching (that is once we got her away from punching walls!), and even binge eating for comfort.

Taking Responsibility—Gaining Control

Now when Andrea leaves her room a mess (which is a rare event these days according to Jill, who is enjoying a great deal more respect from her teenager), Jill chooses very different thinking.

She describes this new thinking as follows:

✓ I choose to allow myself time before I respond to things I might interpret as being disrespectful, as I now recognize these are some of my own issues I am trying to overcome. As I respect myself more, others follow.

✓ I choose to remove my self-judgment about my parenting.

✓ I choose to think logically that a messy room does not have to represent a doomed adult life for my daughter.

✓ I choose not to make Andrea's room a complete representation of how she feels about me.

We clearly have a wonderful bond, and even better now that I'm not so fearful.

Both Jill and Andrea continue to work on taking responsibility for their thoughts, feelings and behavior. It is a lifetime journey. Awareness is the first step. Much change occurs naturally just with this first step. Denial is the ego's way of limiting our ability to see our full potential.

The Denial

Jill also relayed to me she was now keenly aware that her willingness to be honest with herself was directly related to the way in which she was learning to treat herself. Coming from love, she discovered how she was responsible, at least in part, for the dysfunctional relationship she and Andrea were dancing in. "If I hadn't had someone reminding me it really was all right to feel frustrated and to get it wrong sometimes, I suspect I might not have wanted to confront myself."

We deny our contribution to an unhappy or unhealthy situation often because we fear our own self abuse!

How I behave in accordance with how I think creates my life. If we continue to think that every perceived negative experience we encounter is someone else's fault, we give away our power to change the life we experience.

EXERCISE 9D

OPPORTUNITY TO GAIN CONTROL OVER DESIRED OUTCOMES

• *Having read Jill and Andrea's story, look around in your own life and see where you feel out of control.*

• *How have you been choosing to gain greater true-self control?*

• *How could you improve the skills you are already using to gain more true power over your own life?*

• *If you feel you suffer from guilt, defensiveness, how might you choose to release it?*

The Ego's Effect on Motivation

Why else might we struggle with sustainable change when we genuinely believe we desire the changes? There are several reasons and these might include such things as:

Fear of Rejection

Fear of Judgment

Fear of Self Abuse

Fear of Failure   **= Fear of Pain—Guided by the ego**

Fear of Success

Fear of Looking Like a Fool

Fear of Not Being good Enough

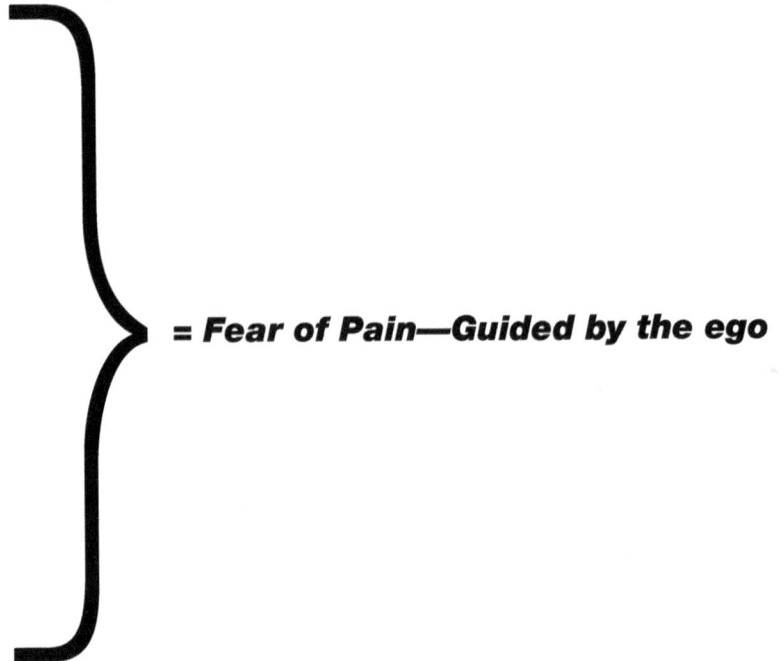

EXERCISE 9E

HOW DO YOU FEAR THE PAIN INFLICTED BY YOUR EGO?

If you had no fear/ego around creating all that your soul desires in this lifetime, your "desires" would not exist because they would simply be your reality. You would think with perfect clarity, feel nothing but gratitude, love and be joyful, and you would generously share these offerings with everyone and everything. (Just quietly between you and me, I suspect you wouldn't require *Permission to Dance* either!)

Be proud of identifying your fear. It takes more courage to confront it than it does to deny it.

1. Make a list of some of the fears that you have relating to creating change in your life, (in addition to the list of seven things on the previous page). If any of these are included in your list, put a tick beside it so you can go back to it for an exercise further on.

Using Pleasure and Pain to Gain Authentic Control

There is nothing we can do that does not carry the intention of one of these two things:

- *The Pursuit of Love* (Pleasure)

- *The Avoidance of Fear* (Pain)

The need to avoid anything that will make us feel fearful is built into our nervous system because it is a natural survival mechanism. However, most of what we fear is an illusion based on history—our own history. For the average person, most of our anguish is quite unnecessary and manufactured to protect us from our fear that the past will repeat itself.

Our pursuit of love is also based on an illusion, one that says we are not loved already. We must reach out for what we haven't got. It says we are not naturally worthy of being loved and therefore we must do, say, be, and wear all the right things that will make us lovable. So we seek, and we pay and we betray our naturally adorable state.

That old saying that "there is nothing to fear but fear itself" is so very true. The other less popular truth is this:

```
you are lovable today... before the makeover,

before you have mastered mastery...

in the middle of your anger,

you are lovable as you put off until tomorrow

what you have yet to find the motivation to do today,

and even in your limited belief about who you are,

you are lovable today.
```

How the Ego (Fear) Immobilizes Us

Why do today what you can do tomorrow…or the day after…or the day after…? Why do we wait to start our life…tomorrow?

*We **procrastinate** first and foremost because we fear the risk of moving forward. We fear it will be more painful to do something, rather than to do nothing.*

I used to think I was extremely lazy. I came to understand I just hadn't worked out what I wanted to move forward on, so I did everything but that which might serve my own life.

I vividly remember on many cold winter mornings my father opening my bedroom door at some ungodly hour and stating in his usual morning voice, "Time to get up sleepyhead." I would drink in the last minutes of my warm flannelette sheets, protesting the cruelty of making a child get up at dark and travel an hour into the city to endure another day at St. Clements private all girls school. By the second call (because you didn't hang around for the third) my tiny butt would drag itself away from the bed's warmth and I hesitantly put on my "ugly black tunic" ready for another day at what I thought was the worst school on earth because of its lack of boy people. Getting up was agony…and I would put it off as long as I possibly could without getting into trouble. I remember the loneliness and isolation that I felt being the only Maxwell who wasn't thriving at St. Clements. I quietly feared my own "stupidity" and my inability to achieve grades that could compare to my far more focused and (what I perceived to be) more intelligent older sisters.

Then Saturday mornings rolled around. That was my day. Grocery shopping always happened on Friday night so the fridge was full of Coke and chocolate ice-cream and the cupboards contained a fresh box of Coco Pops! (Clearly sugar consumption was not a major concern in the 70's!) Cartoons started at 6 a.m. sharp and I wasn't going to miss a moment of Scooby-Doo or the latest Jackson Five cartoon. Getting up wasn't even noticed. I have no recall of getting out of bed on a Saturday morning. I only remember how much I loved eating my favorite sugar-drenched cereal while being entertained in my own world of cartoons where anything was possible.

Love and fear—these are the details we will most remember. I recall clearly my love of cartoons on the weekends and my fear of being a loser for the rest of the week. Every action we take comes from our need to avoid our fear of pain and our yearning for the pleasure we feel when we are connected to love in its many and varied forms.

When we put things off until tomorrow, we are simply focusing on our fear of the pain that moving forward might cause. We fear that taking action will be more painful than doing nothing. If we want to know the truth about our unlimited ability, we must remember our need to avoid pain is just an illusion created by our ego's need to control in order to maintain its false sense of security.

2. As specifically as you can, identify some ways in which fear is currently limiting you from moving forward in a way that serves your true-self.

discipline? what discipline?
find the inspiration get the leverage

focus on the desired outcome

In keeping with my "rebel without a clue" reputation, I just never seemed to get the idea of doing something that I was completely unmotivated to do! It wouldn't matter if it was exercise, going to a party or doing my homework; I needed to have a reason, and a pretty good one to become engaged.

In junior high I had a gym teacher named Mrs. Wilson (who honored me by allowing me to call her Cheryl once I hit high school. Very exciting stuff at the age of 13!) Cheryl took a particular interest in me both as a young girl trying to grow up and my untapped athleticism, often taking me out of a history class and asking me to contribute something to her programs. I will always remember how important I felt when I heard a call over the PA requesting my presence in the gym office. She asked me to choreograph the dances for the Christmas show in year seven—to this day I love "Jingle Bell Rock" and I remember every corny step of that dance.

Cheryl would take me in her little old VW and we would head off to different schools to perform my dances. We would go to gymnastics competitions, basketball and track and field meets. I always remember feeling like a million dollars sitting beside her in that old car with the stick shift in the middle. That VW was my limousine. I had no problem at all finding the motivation to train for track and field, gymnastics, basketball and of course dancing. I would have jumped as high as Mrs. Wilson wanted me to and run even further.

In the middle of a Canadian winter it was often freezing cold and still very dark as I would get up early to head off to morning gymnastics practice. The heaters at school were turned down low through the night so the gym was often pretty chilly first thing in the morning. If I had focused on the dark, the cold, and the aching muscles too hard when I was in the cozy flannelette sheets of my gloriously warm double bed, it would have been a little more challenging to rise and shine. I chose to focus on the pleasure, not the discomfort.

What we focus on grows. It becomes our motivator. Our focus will motivate us to get up and dance, or to stay between the sheets. One way or the other, whatever we commit our minds to generates our outcomes.

Focus on the desired outcome rather than the cost of getting there. As we focus on the pleasure we will gain, rather than the pain we imagine it will cost, we create a feeling of hope rather than despair.

It is futile to reach for the stars if you focus on the pain found in the stretch!

EXERCISE 9F

LOVE/PLEASURE MOVES US INTO ACTION

1. When you were younger, what did you enjoy doing? When were you completely motivated and joyful?

2. What brings you joy now? What are you doing, who are you with, and where are you when you feel truly alive?

3. Are you doing these things often enough in your life today?

4. When will you next do one of the things that bring you joy that you rarely find time to do or have some other reason that it cannot happen? When will you begin to make it happen?

EXERCISE 9G

IDENTIFY HOW YOU RELATE LOVE AND FEAR TO FITNESS

1. Let's look at your relationship with fitness both from the perception of pleasure and from the perception of pain. Finish this list of things that might feel pleasurable to you in relation to obtaining and maintaining fitness.

   Pleasure (A Bi-product of Love/Spirit Self)

   - **Feel more energy**
   - **Feel good about self**

Pain *(A Bi-product of Fear/Ego Self)*

- **Might not be successful at it**
- **Cold outside**
-
-
-
-
-
-

If you want to embrace fitness in your life (and actually maintain it), the trick is to:

1. Make the pleasure list longer than the pain list.

2. Focus only on the pleasure—making it bigger in your mind while making the pain almost insignificant.

3. In any moment when the pain is allowed to sneak in and take over your thinking, turn your focus onto the pleasure list. As you do so, you gradually reprogram your brain to think first of the pleasure rather than the pain until the pain no longer exists as your reality.

More Pleasure

-
-
-
-
-

Watch What You Focus On.

To be inspired is to feel your own essence.

To address that inspiration is to actualize your soul's greatest **yearning.**

I often observe unhappy people setting about to find the discipline to do what they don't want to do in order to achieve something that is the misguided desire of someone else. I just can't help but wonder what the point is in trying to achieve things in our lives if they have nothing to do with how we want to experience this lifetime. Really, what for? Why try to make yourself earn more money if you intend doing it in a way that has nothing at all to do with why you showed up here in the first place? Why not make that money doing something that you love—which will naturally be something you like doing?

No big surprize you are very likely to discover the money wasn't what you were really striving for all along. It was the freedom you feel when you're doing what you love to do! Why try to make yourself *disciplined* enough to stick to something which makes you feel unhappy? Is it not our responsibility to bring the best of who we are to the world? By checking inside we are able to find our natural inspiration, motivation, and our drive to do what it takes to bring to life our passions. This is not a luxury. It is what you came here to do in this lifetime and when you don't do it do what we love to do,

EXERCISE 9H

OPPORTUNITY TO FOCUS ON WHAT YOU REALLY DESIRE

I include this exercise on money because my experience is that many people allow the energy that is money to be blocked in their lives and therefore cause limited beliefs about what they can achieve. It is the one thing that most people say they either want more of or they resent it. It is often on the list of things that a person would change when I do my workshops on creating sustainable change. They would either like to have more money or they resent the institutions or the people who have it. The fact is money is currently our society's form of trade. Like all things, depending on the relationship you have with it, money has the potential to serve your spirit's desires, or block them. Let's see how you feel.

Even if your first reaction is that you do not need to do this exercise for whatever reason, it is here for more than one purpose. Give it a try anyway.

Part 1—$$$

- *What does money mean to you? What can it buy? If money is just energy, like everything else, then what does that energy represent to you?*

Personal Example:

For me money represents:

1. The freedom to allocate several hours each week to charity and/or community work without having to worry about my own bills

2. The ability to work for myself thus maintaining control of the integrity with which my business conducts its dealings

3. The ability to fly to places for work or play

4. Etcetera, etcetera…

Part 2—$$$

Identify Your Feelings Surrounding the Energy that is Money

- *What do you feel like when you have all of these "things"? How do you see your life? How do you see your life looking if you had less money? More money?*

Personal Example continued from one of the above answers:

Charity/community work—I gain deep fulfillment when I'm able to help others discover what is possible in their lives and I'm grateful I am at least in part, able to experience this mutual exchange not limited to someone's ability to pay for my services. Not having to charge everyone just to survive means I get to meet and share with various individuals who turn out to be the most inspiring people I've ever met and I might never have met them if everything was about just being able to survive financially.

Okay your turn…

What does money really mean to you?

When I have the things in my list above, I feel:

What's $$$ got to do with Unveiling My True-Self?

I used money as one example because so many people think it will help them find greater happiness. I believe because we trade in money in our society, it does allow us to experience certain things more easily. But I also know from my own experience and that of so many others that money in itself is not what we want.

If we take the list I used above as an example, before I was able to allocate several hours each week to charity and/or community work without worrying, I did it anyway, and I found a way not to worry. Before I could self publish, I learned the power of manifesting my deepest desires until I created a way that I could. Before I could fly my son to visit me, we drove. Before I could take Jess, my daughter, out whenever I wanted to, she learned that like her mother, she wanted to earn money in ways that made her feel good about herself. Before I could talk to overseas friends and family whenever I wanted to, I made sure I valued every moment of the time we did have together.

I did not feel hard done by! I knew it wasn't about the money; it was about growing, learning and choosing happiness regardless of whatever I was experiencing. I was then more able to understand what it was I desired at a core level. In this way, I discovered what inspired me.

Rather than asking for more money, I asked to be open to my own creative ways in which I could experience more time with my family, more opportunities to work with inspirational clients, and the wisdom to know when opportunities were being presented to me.

HOW I FEEL ABOUT THE EVENTS IN MY LIFE

IS MORE IMPORTANT TO MY HAPPINESS

THAN HAVING WHAT I THINK I WANT!

EXERCISE 9I

FINDING AND EXPERIENCING WHAT YOU REALLY DESIRE

Identify five things you really want to experience in your life that you currently are not experiencing.

This activity is heightened when done with a willing and playful partner. Find someone else who is supportive. It is important you feel safe and can have fun with this. It still works if you choose to practice this one alone.

> **General Examples:**
>
> 1. I want to experience having a better relationship with my brother
> 2. I want to experience being a non-smoker
> 3. I want to experience having a happy relationship with a partner
> 4. I want to experience joy in my work

- **I want to experience and/or change:**

    (Write the most important one first. If you did this thing or made this change, it would have an altering effect on your entire life.)

    i

    ii

    iii

    iv

    v

EXERCISE 9J

CREATING THROUGH MEDITATION

- Take time for a gentle meditation, relaxation, prayer and/or visualization. As we sit in peace, we allow ourselves the best possible opportunity to listen to our inner voice of wisdom.

- If you have a partner to play with, possibly one could lead the other in a relaxation, or you could read the "Candle Meditation" out loud to each other. If not, try visualizing a place that feels very safe and extremely peaceful for you. Put on a guided meditation or music you find relaxing.

- Check in with your inner wisdom and ask where your intention is. We can think we want something that might in no way meet our true and deepest desires. Are these wants coming from your spirit or your ego?

EXERCISE 9K

ASK FOR CLARITY RELATING TO YOUR SOUL'S DEEPEST DESIRES

• Following the meditation, are you sure this is really what you want to experience?

If you have felt, seen, heard or acknowledged anything else your soul is asking for, please note it down here:

EXERCISE 9L

BUILDING THE MOTIVATION TO MOVE

Gain Power Over Your Ego

Many people write lists of things they want or do not want in their lives; however, their lists are not truly representative of their own desires. Often we are so conditioned to do, think or feel in a way others might approve of, we lose sight of what is important to our own lives. Focus only on what you want, not what you think you should want. *Should* is a word well loved by the ego. It keeps you victim through carefully set out imaginary rules that usually relate to someone else's life rather than your own.

1. Write down 10 reasons why you absolutely must experience item #1 on your list of five things. Do not quit until you find 10 reasons.

2. What is the fear or pain you link to these things? Fitness example:

- I've been "bad" because I've ignored it for so long and thinking about it is a reminder

- I might not be able to achieve real fitness

- I might look fat in my gym gear!

The fear/pain I attach to item #1 on my list is:

3. What pleasure (perceived sense of love and/or nurturing) have you received by not doing it? Fitness example:

- I got out of doing something healthy and disciplined

- I got to eat chocolate instead of salad

*The pleasure I relate to **not** doing item #1 in my list in Exercise 9 is:*

4. Write down the outcomes if you do not do or change this thing in your life. Fitness **example**:

- Ill health

- Overweight

- Feeling lousy

*The Outcomes of **not** doing it are:*

5. What will be the positive outcomes if you do item # 1 on your list above? Fitness example:

- Better health

- More energy

The pleasure I relate when I do item #1 in my list in Exercise 9 is:

6. Repeat the same activity for each of the three items on your list of things you would like to change in your life. You can add as many reasons to your list as possible. The more you flesh it out, the more leverage you are gaining over your persistent ego voice (the limiting voice of fear).

···✱ɲℴ♡ℯɲɲℴ✱···

Creating New Beliefs—To Experience Your Grandest Visions For Your Life

While we might think it is our conscious mind that rules our lives, it is in fact for the most part our subconscious mind that processes information and determines how we are going to react to incoming information. The subconscious then feeds a call to action to the conscious mind that results in an action (or many millions of actions) in the body.

Our subconscious mind processes all incoming stimuli through its own unique system. This system has been developed through the storage of past experiences. The greater the state of emotional charge during that past experience, the more powerful the cellular memory will be, and the more your subconscious will use that information to process present information.

This is why we need to create new meaning for past painful experiences. We cannot simply ask our bodies or our minds to *just forget about it* and *pretend* we don't have a cellular memory. This concept of *just getting on with it*, which might often be disguised as *positive thinking*, simply does not work. I should clarify that statement. Positive thinking in itself is a wonderful tool in the process of healing and it might work by itself if your intention is simply to act as if the thinking, feeling and the behavior do not exist within you. However, if you are choosing to create holistic, sustainable change and healing, you must allow yourself to feel more than just positive.

You can be sure your body remembers every tiny, seemingly insignificant experience you have ever had and it will feed that information through to your subconscious whether you like it or not.

The Six Lane Highway To Outcomes

The brain's pathways allow the most rapid response to incoming information. When you really think about it (pardon the pun), your brain is pretty busy! It has a lot to contend with providing a response to every single piece of information that comes its way—small and large.

For example, in this very moment, my amazing brain is telling each finger on my keypad exactly where to go, what to write, how to say it in order that it will be understood (I hope), all the while reminding me that it must be time for lunch. It is doing thousands of other things at the same time, most of which I am not at all conscious of, in the mysterious place called the subconscious.

The more often we respond in a particular way to incoming information, the deeper that pathway gets etched into our brain. I think of this *deep* pathway as a **Six Lane Highway.** It is the fastest route to your destination (an outcome). It is subconscious actions that can make one assume we are defenseless against this control mechanism called our brain. Actually, the opposite is true. Our brain is merely a wonderful tool that provides choice. And when we choose not to choose at all, we are being controlled by external factors.

If you have ever had a physical addiction you will easily understand the concept of the **Six Lane Highway** and how we often do things before we have consciously processed the outcome. Addictions come in many forms however. They can be as subtle as a constant attraction to negative thinking or they may be more obvious as in physical addictions.

CASE STUDY *(Names have been changed for the protection and privacy of my clients.)*

> *Brigitte was a two-pack-a-day cigarette smoker. She came to me saying she wanted to quit but didn't trust herself to do so. She feared if she were not successful at letting go of the habit, she would plunge into an even worse place of self loathing. Cigarettes were affecting her health, her relationship with a new non-smoking partner, and most importantly, her self-image and self-esteem.*

The Initial Decision to Create a New Positive Pathway

Together Brigitte and I started down the road to a new outcome. She decided that now was the time to take the plunge into *the path of her heart*—the healthy, happy, empowered road she knew would lead her to feeling much better about herself and allowing her to have a better relationship with her own body...and the new man! She said, "If I can do this...I honestly believe I can do anything!"

How *empowering* this process would be—and of course, how *challenging*. Her ego knew only too well the level of freedom Brigitte would experience once this limiting behavior no longer had a hold on her, so it wasn't going to give up easily!

Incoming Information

Brigitte described how her mouth would water as soon as she saw the golden cigarette packet that consciously she believed would eventually kill her. But in that moment of craving, when she was more powered by the subconscious need, she would feel frustrated with herself as she craved a cigarette more than her next breath! In that moment, the new relationship would simply be justified—this new partner was going to have to understand her needs! Her heart problems and self-image suddenly seemed impossible to overcome. The incoming information to her brain in that moment was a golden packet, the fear that she might not ever be free of this addiction and *frustration* with herself for being so weak as she put it.

Her brain did what it had been doing for the past fifteen years...

"Ok folks, we need extra saliva down here. What's happening with the right hand over there? Move it! Move it! Excellent. Reaching now for the golden packet. Thank you well done. Lighter in left hand, great…thumb get moving I haven't got all day for you to light up! Okay now lungs—take it in! Yes! My work here is done." Before Brigitte knew it she was smoking a cigarette. But that was in the past.

The First Steps

The simple act of making a conscious choice, further powered by seeking help to achieve her goal, was enough to start a new pathway in her brain. Temporarily at least, Brigitte felt a new power that was coming from listening to and acting upon her highest vision of who she was. The action created the first tracks on her road to a positive outcome.

Replacing the Constant Craving

There were many other strategies we used however the key contributors to supporting Brigitte's success in reaching her positive outcome and creating a new pathway in her brain she says were these two things:

1. Focusing on her success—regardless of falling off the wagon from time to time

"When I got the cravings, I told myself how proud I was of myself so far. I was making a huge effort to create a new life for myself. I focused on the part of myself I liked and I *acted as if* I were a non-smoker. In the first few weeks when I snuck the odd cigarette, I would remind myself that I'd been doing really well and I *would not punish myself with negative thoughts or words* but rather focus on how far I had already come and how bad my mouth tasted when I did have the odd puff—knowing it simply didn't suit the new non-smoking me to have bad breath!"

2. Do something different—every time.

"I learned the idea of giving something up was equal to a punishment in my *child mind* so we had to find replacements. My cigarettes were my way of taking *time just for me* so I chose to give this to myself in ways that served my desired outcome, to quit smoking and feel good about myself.

I can look at anyone smoking the sticks in that golden packet now and since creating new pathways in my mind, I am left with only the memory of bad breath, heart palpitations and asthma! It has been three years now! Never again."

Notes:

The Six Lane Highway:

In this example, the arrow to the right indicates repeating the negative cycle over and over. The more Brigitte smoked, the more she craved. The more she craved, the more she smoked. That was before she made the decision to create a new path that lead to positive outcomes.

Negative habits are recreated so we might choose to release them. Positive habits repeat in order that we might enjoy them. Our outcomes depend on whether or not the Six Lane Highway, or the path of least resistance is of service to us, or it is self-sabotaging.

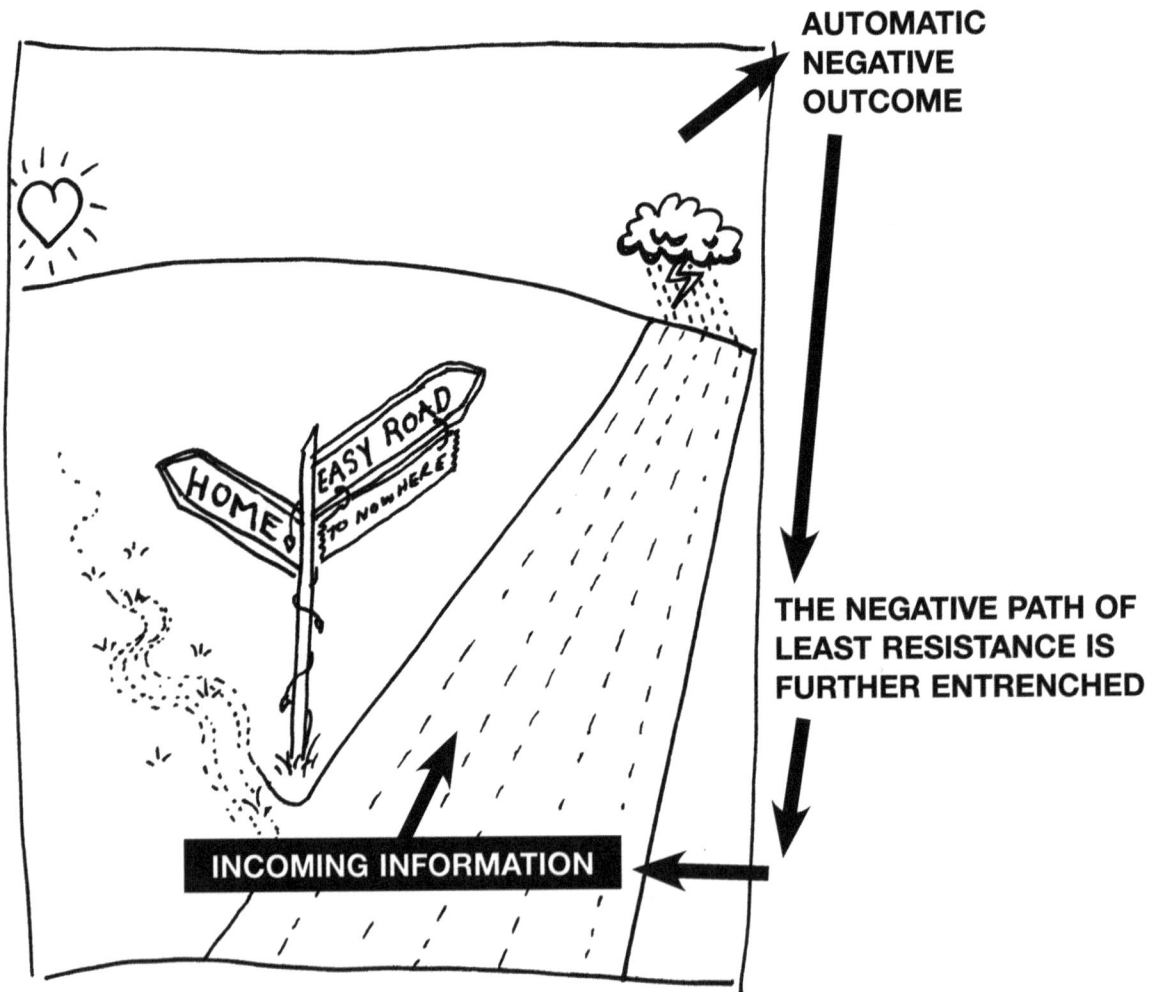

AUTOMATIC NEGATIVE OUTCOME

THE NEGATIVE PATH OF LEAST RESISTANCE IS FURTHER ENTRENCHED

INCOMING INFORMATION

EASY ROAD

HOME

TO NOWHERE

EXERCISE 9M

OPPORTUNITY TO DRIVE ON THE SIX LANE HIGHWAY

We all have old negative habits that are limiting us today. For some people it's easy to identify the behavior and then link it to a belief; however other things that sabotage our connection with our true-self can be more subtle. This is a good time to remember some breathing exercises or refer to the *Permission to Let Go* CD to do a meditation practice.

Once you are in a relaxed state, trust that you are quite capable of identifying some of your own Six Lane Highway messages.

- *What are a few of the behaviors that no longer serve you?*

Changing the Six Lane Highway to a Path of Least Resistance

To create a new habit we must create a new Six Lane Highway that gradually becomes our new path of least resistance. It requires a split second of conscious choice, followed by a little road work that carves the new road to success. This process requires gently placing one foot in front of the other in unknown territory—positive affirmations each step of the way, making consistent choices to resist the urge to self-criticize for perceived *failures,* and acknowledgement of the smallest of steps on the new road. Each positive word, each positive effort is worthy of reward and celebration. You are one step closer to creating your chosen outcomes rather than having the external world dictate how your life will be experienced.

Our Inbuilt Ability to Create New Productive Pathways

I always imagine this process of creating a new pathway to healthier behavior to be a little like making the choice to take a machete and carve a new road in some thick bushy rainforest when the temptation of getting there faster on that Six Lane Highway lies just off to our right.

So here we are. On the one side we have the machete in hand, thick rainforest scrub, fear of things that bite, mosquitoes buzzing around our heads...

On the other side we have a smoothly paved Six Lane Highway, an air-conditioned sports car with mag wheels, and of course all the comforts of knowing where we'll end up. (Even if it isn't where we really want to go, at least we know the destination.)

Making the choice to create a pathway of least resistance in service to the pathway of our heart is just the beginning.

So the journey begins with our choice to take up the challenge. After looking at the pleasure and pain, love and fear ratio, we decide the pain of staying stuck is greater than the pain of embracing this particular positive change in our lives.

We can feel our focus is keenly on the pleasure we will gain by allowing our spirits to lead the way, and we are feeling connected to the part of ourselves which is loving.

It's all looking good so far…

With commitment and machete in hand, the work begins, the temptations start, the perceived (negative) payoffs which serve only to keep you stuck; the people asking you why you need to make changes when they liked you better the old way. Every button that could be pressed seems to be getting a battering. It's raining, the dog eats your Permission Practice Journal, the kids get sick, and your inner voice of fear is hammering in your head like a migraine telling you to

STOP! Can I really do this?

yes you can
and **now** would be a good time to get back on the road!

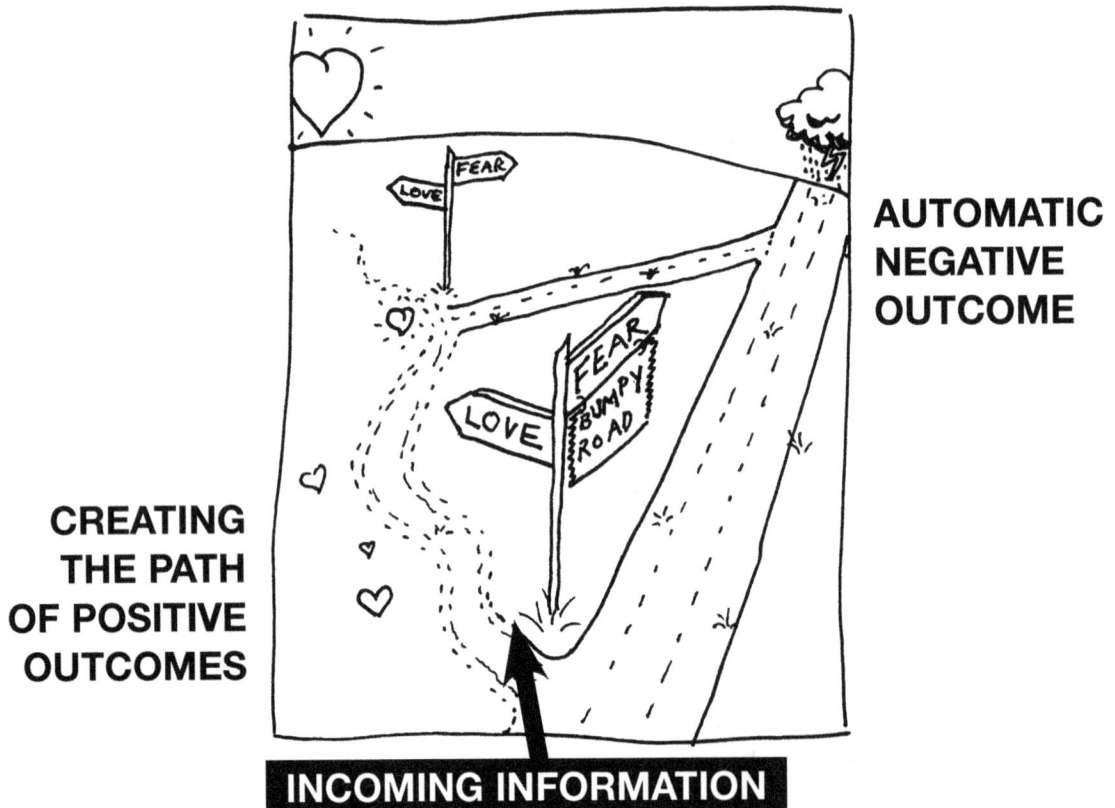

CREATING THE PATH OF POSITIVE OUTCOMES

AUTOMATIC NEGATIVE OUTCOME

INCOMING INFORMATION

EXERCISE 9N

Choose one item from your list of things you want to change or experience (Exercise 9i) that you have some resistance to:

Programming a new pathway

Requires Repetition

and Choice

I have discovered that making a choice to change my focus **from FEAR to** *Love* requires me to refocus—sometimes moment to moment. Particularly in the early days I noticed some mornings I would wake up feeling bothered. It was an old pattern of mine to worry upon waking. I could always find something to stir my previously rested mind. I would worry about anything from how I was going to live up to my full potential to how I was going to pay the rent. I wasn't fussy! Morning was my time to worry. My *second* thought however was to remember I wanted to focus on love today. I can tell you from years of experience, my choice to focus on love is what has changed my life…and the lives of everyone I have taught. It has a wild effect on us!

With this loving focus in hand, heart and mind, in no time at all, I began laughing at myself regularly—oh let's be honest, I still laugh at myself most days as I find myself thinking, feeling and behaving in ways that disrupt my peace. I just laugh. And then I remember. I simply get back up and I start again. More often than not, my choice to focus on love today just *is.* No effort required.

While our new road might not be the path of least resistance initially—as we choose, so shall it be.

I'm following the path of

my heart rather than

the path of least resistance.

Learning how to be kind to ourselves as we fall down on our often fragile little butts allows us the opportunity to create the Path of our Heart while gently, minute by minute, choice by choice, making it the path of least resistance.

The most important part of this entire process of creating new beliefs that generate outcomes consistent with our spirit's desire is that we need to remain loyal to ourselves regardless of how long we do or do not persevere each time. As long as we continue to take responsibility for our choices we've done well. We keep getting further along that path and the path itself continues to get wider, deeper and easier to travel on.

Sit quietly. Take a deep breath. Close your eyes.

- *Recall(within the past week) your inner Voice of Fear. Become aware of what it says and how it effects you. How does your negative inner voice take you off the path of your Heart?*

the path of the *heart*

= the path of least resistance

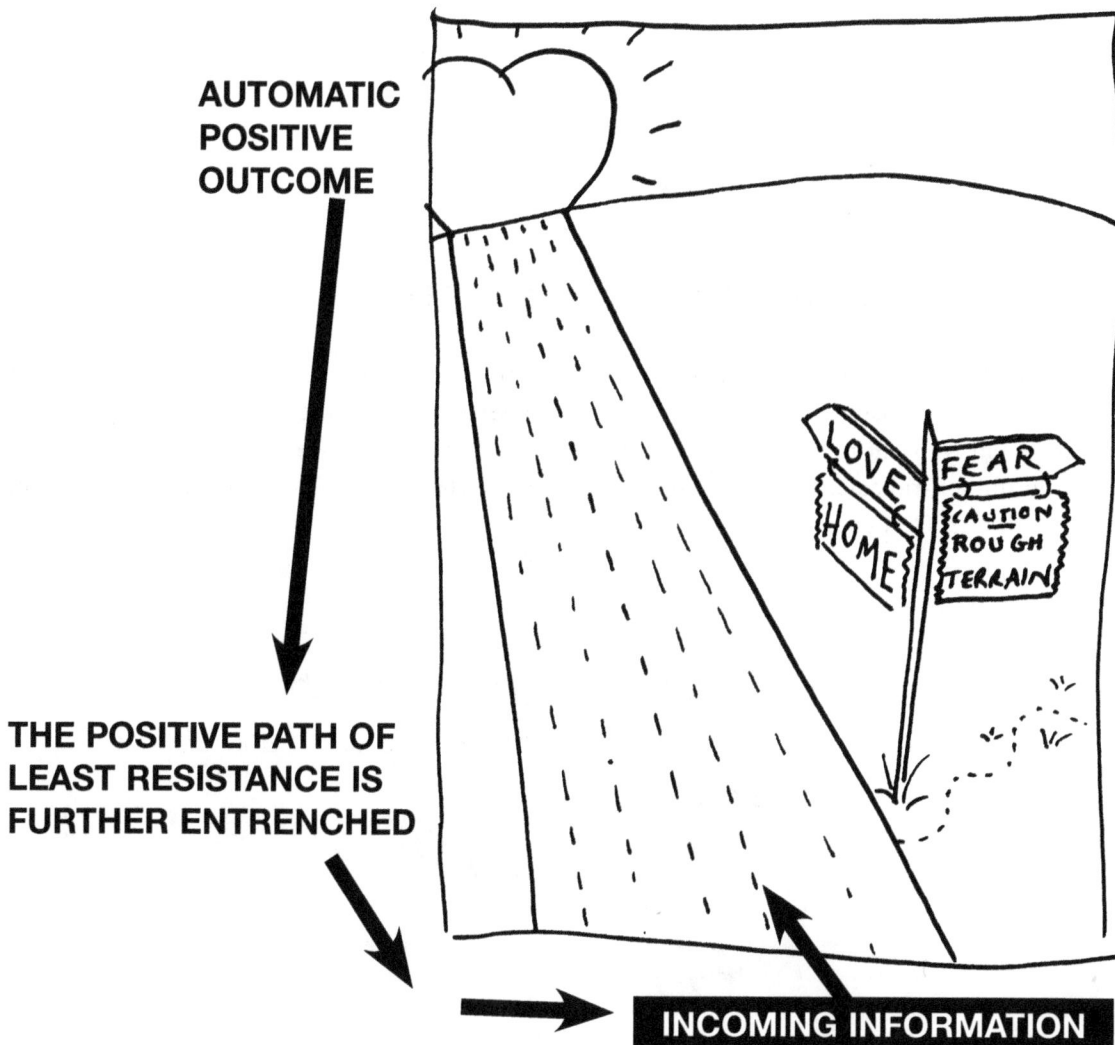

AUTOMATIC
POSITIVE
OUTCOME

THE POSITIVE PATH OF
LEAST RESISTANCE IS
FURTHER ENTRENCHED

LOVE
HOME

FEAR
CAUTION
ROUGH
TERRAIN

INCOMING INFORMATION

the greatest **FEAR** we have

is of what we do
to ourselves
inside our own mind.

The Path of our Hearts is the Path of Unconditional Love

Each time you allow the moment to be pleasurable rather than painful; you affirm to yourself the process of creating this new and positive habit is actually enjoyable, as opposed to it providing yet another reason to be self-critical. Why would we want to subject ourselves to the task of making changes if the process was going to be filled with hurtful self-ridicule? For most people that's exactly what it is. And we wonder why we live in a world so filled with fear! Go figure.

If you find yourself turning right back onto the Six Lane Highway, blow yourself a kiss as you make the turn...and choose to get back on the road!

EXERCISE 90

WHEN THE GOING GETS TOUGH...

This is a great exercise to practice as a good reminder whenever it all seems too difficult. If the road to awakening your full potential never gets challenging for you, you're either one highly evolved dude/dudette or you're not pushing the envelope as much as you could!

For most of us mere mortals, there are days when we simply need a reminder. We can become stuck in past limited thinking, feeling and behavior, which leaves us temporarily immobilized once again. Ebb and flow, up and down, back and forth...it's all part of the Dance of Unveiling. Just keep choosing!

1. Look at what you wrote in the last exercise, (9n) and apply each of the items found in the Creating Change Summary Sheet that follows as well as the guidance below. You can apply these steps to any situation in which you are feeling blocked.

2. Use the blank pages in the back of this book or your own journal to document your process from blockage to unlimited.

3. Put a checkmark next to each item below as you have addressed them.

4. As you go, write down what you discover and how it supports your moving forward.

THE TOUGH GET GOING...

• Use the three R's—Rest, Regenerate, Refocus (Refer to your breathing and meditation notes and/or the Permission to Let Go CD).

• Become aware of how your threatened ego tries to tell you that you have in some way failed because you are struggling. How does it do this to you?

• Write down how you have already been successful in so many ways.

• Be kind to yourself—but keep going!

• Revisit the love and fear (pleasure and pain) tools—focus on the pleasure you will gain by moving forward, step, by baby step, by baby step...what do you discover?

• Re-identify what you might be fearful of, acknowledge the need for more love in that area of your life, be that love for yourself, and in this way you have already naturally moved out of fear—remove the ego's power.

• Revisit what you wrote in the exercises under the heading Gaining Power over Your Ego. Focus on the feelings that support love and use the fear to notify you of a place within that is in need of healing—then let it go once it has served its purpose.

• Remember again why you made the choice to make the specific change(s) you're working on.

• You fell of the wagon? So laugh, lick your wounds and get back on!

Repeat again... and again... and again until the

Path of Your Heart becomes the Path of Least Resistance

Summary Sheet

1 Awareness is the first step to creating positive change.

2 Taking responsibility is the second.

3 What we truly desire at our core and what our ego tells us will make us happy are two different things —it is important to be conscious of where our "desires" originate from. (Ego or Spirit?)

4 Regardless of the story we attach to our desires, in reality we only want to change one or more of these three things:

- Our thinking
- Our feelings
- Our behavior

5 Love and fear are the two core motivators.

6 Focusing on our spirit is the foundation of true inspiration.

7 When we are inspired (in-spirit) we are naturally motivated to move forward.

8 What we focus on grows!

9 Procrastination is caused by our focus being on our fear (pain) related to moving forward rather than the love (pleasure) we will gain by moving in-spirit.

10 If we continue to do what we've always done, we will continue to get what we have always gotten. Choose to do something different.

11 Self-ridicule is one of the key contributors to procrastination and self-sabotage. When we "fall off the path," all that is required is to get back on it, gently, quietly and with love.

6 QUESTIONS

to ask when procrastination sneaks in

1 What is the fear I attach to moving forward?

2 What pleasure do I believe I gain by putting this off?
Be aware of the thing you want to do or stop doing.
What is the perceived gain?

3 What pain have I suffered because I have put this off?

4 Why MUST I make the change and/or create this new beginning?

5 What will I lose if I don't?

6 What will I gain if I do?

10. dancing on the inside

Connecting To Inner Resources

How much do you allow the external world to dictate how you will feel today? How connected and aware are you of your available internal power? Together we are going to observe your internal and external resources and how much you rely on each.

EXERCISE 10A

IDENTIFY INTERNAL AND EXTERNAL RESOURCES

1. This exercise is most enjoyable when shared with a partner. Have them read this scenario to you out loud and slowly as you close your eyes and imagine. Try to answer the questions below as honestly as you can. If you're doing this activity alone, allow yourself plenty of time to absorb the feelings as you read.

You are driving to the office...

You drive to work with the windows down to enjoy the perfect temperature of a summer morning. You are running 15 minutes later than usual because the alarm clock didn't go off. You pull up to what feels like your tenth red light when you have only traveled eight blocks. You hear the sounds of teenagers swearing at one another as they laugh at full volume. A loud truck pulls up beside you and you smell the pungent fumes. An airplane just took off from the airport and flies low overhead. You hear the last few words of the radio announcer's voice, saying something about a traffic accident on the highway as you turn and enter the freeway ramp. It is clear sailing for the first 500 meters and then you see what might best be called the freeway "parking lot." Traffic is banked up for as far as your eyes can see. Your hand reaches for the mobile phone and dials the office to notify reception you will be late for your first meeting. The receptionist is not in yet. Your only hope of having someone greet the important client who was to meet you at 8:30 has just vanished before the same eyes that are right now looking at a sea of auto chaos.

How are you traveling so far?

How do you feel at different parts of the drive?

1.   Describe the parts of the drive that frustrate you most.

2.   What do you notice most and during what part of the drive?

3.   What did you think about?

4.   What did you do?
      (e.g., turn on the radio, call people on your mobile phone, practice breathing exercises?)

5.   What do you think you will focus on during your final 40 minute drive to the office? Be as honest as you
      can. There is no wrong answer.

6.   How do you feel when you arrive late at the office?

Identify some internal resources available to you. In the example above you might have chosen to access such internal resources as these:

- **Love** of music: You could play a good CD or sing out loud at the top of your lungs while stopping at the red lights, as I often do. (I get some looks but I'm pleased to say most people tend to laugh, give me the thumbs up or bop along with me. We get to share a smile and a moment of connection).

- **Faith:** You might put your focus on your faith that all things can be used to serve the highest purpose.

- **Meditation:** Choose to practice breathing exercises. (The highway is a great place to keep your eyes open so I suggest you stay away from deep inner child visualizations!)

- **Connection:** You might choose to smile at another driver who is sharing your experience.

These are just some examples of internal resources. Describe how you might experience these things and add more to the list above. As we do this we become more aware and thus more able to be empowered in times when our buttons are being pressed.

EXERCISE 10B

OPPORTUNITY TO BECOME MORE AWARE OF INTERNAL RESOURCES

How did you respond to the external stimuli in your morning? Would your response best be identified as spirit supportive or ego supportive?

Were you dependent on the traffic? The radio? The alarm clock? Your mobile phone? Your car? The traffic lights?

EXERCISE 10C

FINDING YOUR CORE—MEDITATION

Read this activity and then close your eyes for a moment. Feel free to record the words below and play them back to yourself as your own guided meditation or alternatively listen to the "Candle Meditation" on the Permission to Let Go CD.

Meditation

Letting go of perceived control—accessing true control

Focusing on your breath, allow your focus and your breath to move down into your center, just below the belly button. Breathe in deeply, each time taking your attention to the tip of your nose. Feel the cool air passing in through your nostrils and filling your body, your mind and your essence with pure while light. Each time you let go of the air, feel any change in sensation, focusing again on the tip of your nose. With every breath you become more relaxed, more willing to receive unconditional love and complete acceptance. Breathe in love. Breathe out any fear, pain, frustration, judgment or confusion that might be blocking your ability to fully immerse yourself in your spirit.

EXERCISE 10D

VISUALIZATION

Once you feel relaxed, imagine the last two days of your life as a movie being played on a large screen behind your eyes. Allow the stories to occur, the players to play their parts, and allow yourself to be the star of the show. Try not to judge but just observe.

Once you are able to observe without needing to judge, ask yourself the following two questions:

1. How do I currently experience my internal true-self?

2. How do I want to further experience the truth about myself?

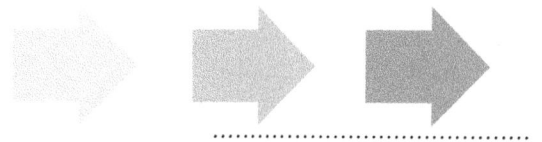

You will be able to open your eyes to write your responses and then close them again to continue asking the questions. You are simply going into your core to discover the truth about the way you experience love.

I find that allowing as much time for this exercise as possible and only doing this one activity for the day helps to make it more concrete. There is no need to rush the process and you can revisit this exercise as often as you like. I must have done this one visualization hundreds of times as I strive to access my internal resources when my *sore spots* want to dictate my outcomes...often winning the game before I've even noticed!

1. How do I currently experience my internal true-self?

2. How do I want to further experience the truth about myself?

Internal true-self (resources)	How I already experience	How I want to further experience
1. Self-acceptance		
2. Self-love		
3. Hope		
4.		
5.		

It's just a dance
But it's **your** dance
and only you can make it beautiful

They say there's no dance rehearsal in this show called life

I don't know so much.

As I dance... it's just one big fancy dress rehearsal, discovering where I fall down,

improving,

awakening

and the show goes on

Regardless of whether I practise, or fall, improve or awaken
So I choose simply to enjoy the act of dancing.

11. the victim versus the empowered

The Blame Game

To get to a place in which we might choose to live empowered by our true selves, we must first decide to stop dancing around the blame game. As we try to find fault, blame and accusations, we miss the opportunity to take responsibility for our own thoughts, feelings and behavior; it is only as we acknowledge our own contribution that we can gain true control over our own lives.

It is not what people do to us that hurt us.
*In the most fundamental sense it is **our chosen response***
to what they do to us that hurts.

– Steven R. Covey

THE VICTIM

When we are playing the victim, we blame undesirable outcomes on things such as these:

*   **The stories of childhood:** "I can't have a healthy relationship because I never had an example of what one might look like when I was growing up."

*   **What is going on around us:** "I would be a lot more understanding if he would just stop being such a pain in the butt!"

*   **Lack of ability:** "I would do it differently if only I could but I don't have the courage that you have."

*   **Social conditioning:** "That's just the way it is in society these days. Nothing I can do!"

*   **Family inheritance:** "Uncle Joe had a bad temper so I got it from him."

THE EMPOWERED

When we are empowered, our spirit self guides through:

- Self-awareness

- Self-acceptance

- Awareness and acceptance of those around us

- Taking responsibility

- Contribution and observation within our relationships

- Choice—to act according to our true-self

- Focus on the present moment (past does not = the future)

- Use of any situation to grow in connection to truth and spirit

WATCH YOUR LANGUAGE

As we choose to take control of our lives in a fundamentally healthy way, it becomes important to listen to the messages we give ourselves about creating what we desire.

The language of love	**The language of fear**
I choose to	I have to
I can	I could if only...
I could if I want to	There's nothing I can do
I acknowledge my feelings as messages from my Spirit; they do not control me	*She makes me so angry!*

EXERCISE 11A

OPPORTUNITY TO BECOME MORE AWARE OF THE LANGUAGE YOU USE

1. Pay particular attention to the language you use in relation to creating what you desire in your life. See how your ego tries to tempt you into the false victim belief that the outside world dictates your experience.

- Today I noticed that my language was:

- And I felt:

- In relation to:

- So I:

- And I felt:

- My inner wisdom was telling me:

EXERCISE 11B

IDENTIFY THE SORE SPOTS—ERADICATE THE AUTOMATIC RESPONSE

Within each of us lie invisible "sore spots" that have been created through painful or uncomfortable experiences. Many of these wounds were inflicted before the time of our most distant memory of childhood so our responses to certain situations could seem irrational, childish and unlike our adult self. That's because they are. They are based on old stories that have been stored in our cellular or subconscious memory and they have nothing to do with now.

1. Identifying your "sore spots" and knowing what responses they activate in you.

    Make a short list of some of the situations, people, and stories that create a negative automatic response for you.

What is going on around you?

How are you feeling?

Who and what is in the picture?

Focus and Intention

The ego will not be happy you have decided to continue your focus and intention to know yourself more lovingly. It will try to hide your *sore spots* from view because as long as you stay wounded, blind to your own power to create different outcomes, your ego self can safely exist. If your spirit-self starts to gain too much headway, a part of the ego self must die, and that's not a trip any self-respecting ego wants to take.

Relax

The things that cause you to have a negative automatic response can be very subtle so once again allow yourself to sit quietly and focus gently on the past two weeks with this question as your intention and focus.

EXERCISE 11C

WHAT'S THE STORY? WHAT'S THE RESPONSE?

It is quite acceptable in our society to place blame on others for our own fearful behavior, which is partially why it can be so challenging to change. It is a small minority who choose to at least *try* to access love in times of attack.

Capital punishment is a classic and extreme example of an eye-for-an-eye mentality. "We wouldn't have to kill them if they didn't break the law!" The very same people who pull the switch or provide the lethal injection swear on the bible to tell the whole truth and nothing but the truth, so help them God—a bible that clearly states, "Thou shalt not kill." It does not say, "Unless people break the law." Many aspects of our legal systems, our politics, our business practices and our teaching children to punch back are all founded on the same automatic response, which stems from fear. On many levels we are conditioned to believe that not taking responsibility for our own responses is acceptable depending on the "story."

To truly give ourselves Permission to Dance, we must think differently. By taking full responsibility for our actions, we become empowered to make choices. Action without thought (*our own* thinking not that of others), can incite dangerous outcomes.

What presses my buttons?

Provide four recent examples.

The Story (situation)	The Automatic Response
1.	1.
2.	2.
3.	3.
4.	4.

Now identify how you would choose to respond to each situation if you were accessing your internal resources.

The Story (situation)	The Automatic Response
1.	1.
2.	2.
3.	3.
4.	4.

As I take responsibility for my response
to other people and the situations around me,

I become empowered to make choices based on my true-self ...

not my fearful-self who has been conditioned
by other people's belief systems.

I stop putting myself down for the negative
patterns that I have created.
I understand that in the past I did these things
because I believed I was less worthy than I am.

Today I choose to change those beliefs!

I am dealing with thoughts

And thoughts can be changed.

I am not powerless to my thoughts.
I create and control them.

I take my own power back and release
the negative old ideas about myself
I feel good about myself for the choices I'm making!

12. finding joy (somehow she got lost!)

This week your entire focus is on **joy.** What a way to spend a week! Regardless of your activities this week, our task together is to stay focused on the joy you gain from any given moment.

At first it might seem ridiculous, impossible, frustrating and downright silly. But if you continue to practice the concept of finding joy in the moment, I can promise you, you can find it.

Example:

Last week one of my major tasks was to research taxation material for a non-profit organization I'm involved in. Can you guess where I might put taxation on my own joy list? Let me tell you it's somewhere right in-between having a tooth extracted without a local anesthetic and having my pubic hairs plucked . . . very slowly! (Not that I have tried either and I certainly have no intention of doing so in the near future.)

However I knew if I wanted to enjoy the day—and I always choose to do at least that—I would have to use this task as an opportunity to practice conscious conditioning: what you focus on grows. I knew the more I would tell myself what a lousy task this would be, the more lousy the task would be, and I would be putting myself at risk of being subjected to an unnecessarily lousy day. In fact, it was quite possible I would avoid the task all together (refer to everything you've learned about procrastination), and I would miss out on an opportunity that was important to my own development and that of the organization. I wasn't willing to risk that negative outcome, so my choice was to focus on the joy I would gain as I discovered the possibilities available to the organization. I chose to immerse myself in the moment and feel good about myself as I discovered my ability to process and understand this sometimes complicated information. I had spent the best part of that day involved in very intellectual processing that I would say rates much further down the joy list than a day of creating, writing, public speaking, or seeing clients. The deal was, it had to be done. So I chose to do it in joy.

*Your challenge this week is to place your focus on the moment to find the **joy.***

Hey! I found Joy. →

JOY!

EXERCISE 12A

A WEEK OF JOY—DAY ONE

You have already written a joy list, but today is a new day and you can never have too many lists of things that bring you joy!

Once again without stopping, write for five minutes a list or an essay about when you feel joy. What is around you? What are you doing? Who are you with? What colors do you feel around joy? There is no limit to what you can write about. Use another page if this space is insufficient. The heading is simply:

Some of the things that bring me joy…

EXERCISE 12B

A WEEK OF JOY—DAY TWO

- Now you have a clearer idea of what brings you joy. When, where, how, with whom and why will you have these things in your life? Yesterday's writing has provided you with a list of your top five joy items.

- List these things again below. You can never have too many reminders!

- Beside the list set a deadline of when you will experience these things—and one of them must be within the next 24 hours. If your joy list only involves "big" things such as winning a million dollars or driving down Route 66 in a red Lamborghini, try to look for some simpler things in which you can find immediate joy.

  For example, if you wrote down "the color blue" as something that brings you joy, this might be an easy one to achieve today. Write today's date and go put on your favorite blue jeans. (Feel free to check yourself out in the mirror too if the mood hits!)

  If, however, you wrote "overseas travel" and you have commitments or current financial limitations that do not allow that to occur for the next 12 months, write down on the right side of the page the date upon which you will be departing at the international airport. Tomorrow we will start the action plan—unless of course you're tempted to start today!

Joy	When?
1.	/ /
2.	/ /
3.	/ /
4.	/ /
5.	/ /
4.	/ /
5.	/ /

Planning a week of joy—exercises for days 3 to 7

The following 10 things to do with your joy list might take you several days to mull over and play with. Take your time, but take action. Remember the more you practice these exercises daily, the sooner you are creating new pathways in your brain that affirm your worthiness of unconditional love. Practice this truth daily, one tiny step at a time.

1. Take your entire joy list from day one and rate each item in level of importance to you.

2. Beside this list, rate your perceived level of difficulty in achieving these things in your life.

3. Take each item and list the perceived obstacles starting with the item you rated as the most difficult to have in your life, and finishing with the item you feel is most achievable.

4. Take your list to a friend or family member who you know most wants to see you in a state of happiness. Insure this person is usually a positive influence in your life. Ask them to challenge your perceived obstacles by helping you to find some solutions.

5. Now take the list and ask yourself on a scale of 1 to 10, how much do I want these things in my life?

6. Write down why you must have the top five things that bring joy into your life.

7. What will you gain if you do?

8. What will you lose if you don't?

9. Finally, take action. Do at least one thing every day that brings you closer to having each and every thing you have on your joy list.

10. Finally look at any perceived obstacles you may have left and apply the following affirmation:

If I think I can, that will be my truth.

If I think I cannot, this also will be my truth.

My choice today is to focus on what I truly desire

at the highest level of what my life can be.

As I make choices in line with my soul's deepest desires

My life becomes aligned with joy.

gradually you will become more confident

that life *was* meant to be easy

and it was certainly meant to be filled with

13. Who do you think you are?
because what you think — you are!

Remembering the gifts that are naturally yours...

You are the contents of the purest gift

wrapped in glossy paper,

not yet opened.

Never feeling the warmth of the sun but through the tiny cracks.

The contents remain unchanging, beautiful and rich in offering

but the wrapping fades and fears its ever changing appearance.

Believing that it is the whole gift.

Open...and allow yourself to be received.

The "Too" Syndrome

I lived much of my life believing that denying my unique gifts meant I had character. In fact, I saw many of my gifts as liabilities rather than assets. I believed that I was *too* everything. I even confirmed this truth by inviting all the perfect dancers into my life who would insure I never forgot just how "too" I really was! They did their job exceptionally well. Without knowing it, they gave me the greatest gifts.

I was *too* outgoing, *too* idealistic, *too* sensitive, *too* much of a dreamer, *too* analytical, *too* childlike, *too* animated and expressive, *too* deep and complicated, yet *too* quick to simplify what is essentially, complicated, *too* quick to assume people are all basically good, *too... too, too, too!*

Gradually with much awareness, affirmation work and self-nurturing, this no longer rang true for me. My inner voice of love was getting stronger and the old thoughts, based on fear, seemed to be losing the battle.

I started to question whether it might actually be a gift to have a belief in the goodness of humankind. Maybe I could use my childlike idealism and dreams to make some changes to my life and to my world.

Since one of my natural passions involves heightening awareness and supporting the release of perceived limitation in myself and others, my sensitivity would be put to good use. I am not ashamed to cry with someone as I see the beauty that they offer in their joy and their pain.

My desire to make a positive difference continued to grow, and I needed to be able to sort through the intricacies of such a task. For this, the universe gave me an understanding of how to take what the world has made complicated, and simplify it so it is more manageable. I am grateful that I have been created outgoing, animated and expressive enough to fulfill my soul's desires. I now understand that denying my talents and special qualities only acts as a block to my being able to best contribute to the world in which I live. I was created exactly as I am, so that I could be exactly who I am. In doing so, I fit perfectly into this wonderful universal puzzle—exactly as I am.

I believe that nothing is without purpose. If we have a quality, we should acknowledge, honor and love it. Whether it be something we recognize ourselves, or something almost invisible to us, like the way we smile that seems to infect others with joy…love it! Denial is not a synonym for humble. It is in this case, more closely related to words such as "blocking the flow of life."

Our unwillingness to receive a gift is equally an unwillingness to give. You cannot give your gifts without first receiving, accepting and honoring them. If you don't acknowledge and accept them, how can you know that you have them to give?

EXERCISE 13A

OPPORTUNITY TO SEE WHO YOU'RE NOT

I call this the Too Syndrome activity and it is one of my favorites to play in a seminar or group environment. One person gives into being the victim of their "too" lies and their partner helps them challenge their ego voice.

If you have someone you can play this with please do. Otherwise, you'll have to just argue with yourself. By now you'll know between our ego voice and our loving voice, we're all pretty much experts at the internal argument anyway!

Make a too list. Write down at least five things you currently say out loud or hear in your voice of fear, which are self-criticisms.

1. I am too

2. I am too

3. I am too

4. I am too

5. I am too

EXERCISE 13B

OPPORTUNITY TO DISCOVER YOUR **UNIQUE GIFTS**

Take each of these self-criticisms and think about how you can put them to good use.

Think about how they are already being used in your life in a positive way and if you are so stuck on seeing them as negative parts of who you are, get help from friends and family. Choose to get assistance with this task from people who you know have historically been a positive influence in your life. These are the people who enjoy watching you grow and are unafraid to share your pain (and their own). If you are unsure whom to do this exercise with, spend some time in meditation and ask to become more conscious of who can support you today.

1. I am   and I'm glad because...

2. I am   and I'm glad because...

3. I am   and I'm glad because...

4. I am   and I'm glad because...

5. I am   and I'm glad because...

EXERCISE 13C

OPPORTUNITY TO USE YOUR GIFTS

I plan to use these gifts in the following ways:

I no longer believe that I am too much or too little of anything at all.

I just am who I am - naturally.

And I am grateful.

EXERCISE 13D

Write a statement you could use to support this truth.

Example:

I am grateful for my sensitivity as I use it every day in my work and home life.

Remember to use this affirming statement whenever you start to think you were given too much or not enough of the qualities that make up the wonderful gift of you.

14. *Love* & self-acceptance... particularly on those **FEAR** days!

Sometimes it is easy to forget we are on a path to self-acceptance and self-love. We all have days when it feels challenging to maintain healthy thoughts, choices, behavior and intentions. On those days, remember your ego is simply taking control and trying to convince you that you are less than who you really are. I find it particularly useful to be gentle on myself on those days, choosing to congratulate myself for the smallest of positive movement forward.

We don't have to be filled with peace, love and joy every minute of every day to be in the process of growing more in love. Acknowledge the small and the large achievements. A small achievement might be something like choosing to smile when you feel down or choosing to pat yourself on the back rather than treat yourself disrespectfully. *You are a work in progress—be supportive*

EXERCISE 14A

ALLOW YOURSELF TO BE A WORK IN PROGRESS

This affirmation is to be used as a reminder that you are making many new choices and it is only your frightened ego voice who will try to make you feel self-defeated sometimes. Reward the *effort* that makes up every tiny baby step you take during the process of your own unveiling!

Today I congratulate myself for choosing to_____ instead of allowing my self-defeating ego voice to convince me there is no point.

Some days it seems really hard to feel like moving forward on my road to self-acceptance and self-love. For me, today is one of those days.

I know I am allowed to have these days, and I congratulate myself for making an effort.

What is Self-love anyway?

The intention of this book is to provide support for those of us who have a habit of forgetting we are completely, amazingly, absolutely lovable…right now. And that we are worthy of love even during our process of being angry, hurt, frightened and the multitude of other feelings that are often judged as less than appealing. Like so many people in this frightened world, I had never felt truly unconditionally loved in my life, so I found it very difficult to know what that kind of love actually looked like in action. How could I action self love when I simply did not know how? I have heard more times than I can remember from caring friends, therapists, and family the wonderful words, "Stop being so tough on yourself." What nobody ever told me wash…how?

It seems particularly important therefore for me to provide many opportunities for you to understand and practice these concepts of being gentle on yourself as you learn more about your own unique dance. We have been practicing the opposite of love for so long that our brains require much reprogramming in order to release the old negative thought patterns and assume more positive truths about the love we are and that we are worthy of receiving.

I have found myself telling a lot of clients to practice "falling in love with you." Allow yourself to play with the bubbles in a bath, make some bubble moustaches and beards like you did as a kid (well, I did anyway) and after all that, dress up in the finest clothes in your wardrobe and take yourself out on a date. It might sound silly, but then I wonder how you can know what great company you are if you spend little time truly *being* with *you?* How can you know how beautiful it is to touch your skin if you've never felt it, or know the magic of your own voice if you never actually listen? In order to know who we really are, we must learn to be both the giver and the receiver, the gift and the hands that embrace it.

EXERCISE 14B

OPPORTUNITY TO DANCE IN SELF-ACCEPTANCE AND LOVE OF THE VESSEL

Become aware of your body. Write down your observations.

1. Falling in love with this vessel called your body is falling in love with the gift of life itself. How could you experience this world if not for the vessel?

2. Hold out your left arm and gently run your right hand over your skin. Try to focus only on the right hand—the hand that is touching your arm. (Of course you can apply this to any body part that might enjoy your loving touch.) How do your fingers feel? Is your skin soft? Rough? What else do you notice from the perspective of your fingers only?

3. Now try to focus only on your arm, or whatever body part you chose. How does it feel to receive your touch? Is it gentle? Does it feel loving or rushed? What else do you notice about your own touch?

4. Now swap sides of your body. If you were using your left hand to touch your right arm, swap that around and make the same observations. How does it feel to give and receive?

5. Become more aware of which body part (the arm or the hand) feels more like the giver and which feels more like the receiver.

6. How does it feel to give to yourself? Write a few lines about the way your hand felt as it touched your skin. Close your eyes and let yourself feel.

7. How does it feel to be received by yourself?

as I become more aware of the gift that I am

I understand that someone else could find me extremely loveable!

This exercise might seem odd. I have to admit it certainly wasn't something I wanted to get caught doing when I first started to discover the gift of me; it happened quite accidentally one day (just between you and me). It is amazing to discover how beautiful our bodies are when we stop judging them as too fat, too thin, or too anything at all. These bodies have been given to us as vessels that support the discovery of our true-self. Falling in love with the vessel is only honoring the entire journey that is our life. I can vouch for the fact it certainly makes the voyage a lot more beautiful, exciting, honest and of course, sensual.

EXERCISE 14C

PAY ATTENTION TO THE MESSAGES OF YOUR BODY

Continue to explore your body as a vessel over the next week. Try not to judge it or compare it to any other vessel. Nobody else was given your body but you. It is the perfect vessel right at this moment to take you to the truth about who you really are. If you feel the need to be more active, fit or healthy, it is your body that is telling you to move. Thank it for the information rather than beating it up with wise cracks as most people do. If you feel stressed, it is your beautiful body that is reminding you to be gentler with yourself, your time and/or your thoughts. Giving thanks is more suitable than ridicule don't you think?

As you write down your discoveries:

- Try not to abandon the activity for at least the entire week.

- If you do, come back to it when you are ready and continue to practice.

- Falling in love takes time as you know. You and you have only just met with the first touch! Practice makes perfect.

- Explore who you are in your vessel in as many ways as you can.
  Look at yourself through open eyes.
  Feel the clothes against your skin as you never have.
  Smell your skin—before and after the soap!
  Allow it simply to be. Explore you as if you've never met!

- Try to remember to be the observer and not the critic.

With all of the opposing incoming stimuli you receive, it is common to struggle with accepting you are beautiful, amazing, lovable and a gift... just exactly as you are in this moment.

KEEP PRACTICING!

You will find the truth.

And the truth is that you are love.

Body Observations:

Day 1

Day 2

Day 3

Day 4

Day 5

Day 6

Day 7

EXERCISE 14D

WALKING MEDITATION—GRATITUDE IN ACTION

This silent and slow walking form of meditation is practiced by Eastern cultures as a form of being in meditation while still living life in service or action. It reminds us, that being present in each moment of our lives need not be with eyes closed and feet crossed in the lotus position. In fact, that would be a very limited way to live don't you think? (It would be quite difficult to get things done…and oh what we would be missing!)

- Take yourself outside where you can feel the air on your skin and the earth under your feet.

- You might need to get rugged-up for winter; don't let that stop you!

- It is when we truly feel that we remember, and the experience has an impact upon us. (Emotion = your reality.)

- Let yourself feel all the elements.

- Commence walking very slowly. Allow each step to take at least 3-5 seconds.

- The issue of balance is likely to come into your consciousness.

- Gradually you will feel more comfortable walking at this deliberate pace. The calm tempo is important to your conscious, sub-conscious and super-conscious experience.

- Continue to walk for at least 20 minutes to half an hour.

- Nature is a great place for your walk; however walking circles in your lounge room can also be a wonderful experience if this is where you find yourself.

- Allow nothing to get in the way of your constant movement.

There are no limitations, only an ego that is trying to limit your experience of the grandest version of your grandest vision of who you really are.

Enjoy the journey!

As you put each foot on the ground:

- Become more aware of each muscle in your feet.

- Feel the muscles in your legs.

- Focus on your back.

- Become aware of the ground under your feet.

- Pay attention to your body's ability to know exactly how to move together in order to create forward movement.

- Feel your breathing and find a rhythm that feels right to you.

- Allow yourself to be completely immersed in the sensations in your body.

- Acknowledge and send gratitude to every body part you can feel working toward your ability to move in any direction you choose. How blessed you are.

- Document your experience. I discovered the more I do this meditation, the more in love I become.

EXERCISE 14E

MEDITATION—LIFTING THE MOOD

Many of my clients who suffered from depression have found this gratitude meditation to be a good one for shifting gloomy energy. For lifting a heavy mood, I often recommend a slight variation on the walking pace to increase it to a fast walk in order to really get the blood flowing.

Very often when I go for walks with my dog, I do this walking meditation at the same time as getting my exercise. I can decide what I want my attention to be on, be it gratitude, body love, goals, or whatever I'm working on at the time, and I keep that as my entire focus. I repeat a positive affirmation to the rhythm of my walking and my breathing. Sometimes I create one of those marching songs the army uses to train soldiers to go into war zones. There's a reason these guys can endure the horrors they're subjected to. They've been well programmed to do so! In no time at all, your conscious mind won't question these rhythmic rhymes.

Marching and chanting in repetitive tones is just one of the tricks I've learned along the way…and it's another shortcut for those of us who prefer to play our way to success rather than work hard and struggle with discipline. I repeat my chant over and over again for the entire 40 minute walk. It will always include gratitude, (another shortcut to success).

For example, if I'm trying to become more physically fit my meditation might go something like this – (Imagine the army chant.)

Breathe-in for four steps	**Feel the rhythm of each step**
Breathe-out for four steps	**"I'm feelin'good now as I move"**
Breathe-in for four steps	**Feel the rhythm of each step**
Breathe-out for four steps	**"Go, get down, get in the groove."**
Breathe in for four steps	**Feel the rhythm of each step**
Breathe out for four steps	*"Every day I do just a little bit!"*
Breathe in for four steps	*Feel the rhythm of each step*
Breathe out for four steps	*"I'm feeling good now gettin' fit!*

Repeat.

It helps to set realistic goals, making the process by which we achieve them fun or at least enjoyable. Remember the "Pleasure and Pain" motivation tools. We naturally want to stay away from anything we perceive to be painful and move toward that which we perceive to be pleasurable.

Making affirmations rhyme or funny can be quite powerful. Anything your body and mind perceive as joyous can be helpful to ensuring you stay on track with your goal. Imagine how you feel about heading back out for your walk tomorrow and the next day if each time you play with walking meditation it is remembered as a playful and positive experience.

At times I might just say the same one line over and over until another line comes to me. It is not important to make your affirmations "good," only to make it sincere, grateful and positive.

The rhythm of your positive inner language, keeping time with your steps, also helps to solidify the intentions in your mind.

Most of us who practice these active meditations report that it is extremely difficult to maintain negativity when we do this exercise in our day-to-day lives. I particularly like the added benefit that I manage to walk my dog, get in my daily exercise and even throw in my meditation time! Extremely time effective I say!

15. Personal business plan

Who are you being? How do you want to experience your life?

The idea of writing my own personal business plan and mission statement occurred to me after doing some professional development where we were guided through the business planning process and the importance of knowing who we are as a business, where we want to head, where we are now, and working through a strategic plan to bridge the gap between those two places.

Most of this *Practice Journal* has been addressing exactly that in our own personal lives. I hope you have become more comfortable with the art of observing your own life while moving away from the temptation to judge. In this way we are best equipped to step away from the details and we are empowered to focus on what needs to be done to bridge the gap between how we want to co-create and where we are today in any given circumstance.

We are coming to the end of this our first dance together. I thought it might be a good time to summarize what you now know to be true about yourself today. While this will change tomorrow (all going well), and I know that living in the moment is vital to moving to our own guidance, having a strong foundation upon which to dance is also important.

It is interesting to me how important planning is in the business world, and yet the most significant business we will ever manage is our own lives, our family, our relationships—our *Company*. Without these things operating in a happy, healthy manner, how much do we drain or gain from our professional lives? You are the CEO of your own company. Nobody can insure it is functioning in a sustainable, proactive, profitable manner but you.

How would you assess its functionality right now? Are you building positive relationships?

Are there any relationships you feel you need to focus on? Would anyone want to buy into your company? Why? Are you the best company you could be?

In my business planning seminar I was asked such questions as:

- What are the core values of your company?

- What is not negotiable in your company?

- What are the core elements of your company?

- What will your company provide and why?

- What makes your company different from other similar businesses?

- When developing your company, who should be on your core strategic planning team?

The list of questions went on; however, I found these particular questions quite appropriate to developing my own personal plan—that is, *my company*. What does it mean to be in *my company?* In fact I discovered I was unable to write my professional plan without having a solid understanding of my personal core values. How could I know how to run my own business with integrity without having clarity on how I wanted to run my own life? While I had many ideas running around in my head, I had never actually put them down in black and white.

I put that seminar to good use. I turned each business planning question onto myself and started to brainstorm a personal plan for my life. The result was quite astonishing. While I expected to find out a few home truths about myself, I was amazed to discover that after working through the process myself, and then brainstorming the concepts with people I trusted, I instantly became more empowered and confident in my ability to run both my own business and my own life. I suddenly knew what motivated me and what did not. I knew the personality traits in people and in myself that tended to slow me down and those that moved me to dance my most remarkable dances. I was aware of what I wanted to grow and what I wanted to downscale in my life. I could see where I was particularly strong, stubborn, easily frustrated—in summary, where my ego had a field day.

I could also see right there on that document where I shine: my gifts, my strengths, my values and my contributions.

EXERCISE 15A

OPPORTUNITY TO UNVEIL YOUR PERSONAL BUSINESS PLAN:

Begin asking the questions that might be a foundation for your own personal direction.

With the list of questions below, change the connotation of a company from meaning a professional business to meaning you.

Answer the following questions with as much detail as possible. Brainstorm with others. Take your time. Observe yourself with this intention in mind.

1. *What are the core values of your company?*

2. *What is it that you value as a person?*

3. What makes your company different from other similar offerings?

Go back to your exercise on the "too syndrome." Identify your uniqueness.

4. What is not negotiable in your company? Think about your boundaries and your values.

5. What does your company provide and why?

What do you offer the world? Your family? Your friends? What does being in your company provide to others? Why do you provide it? Is it important to you? Is it needed by others? Do you need to give it?

Be clear on why you offer what you offer. I found this one of the most challenging exercises because it can take us into the need to fix versus a desire to share our company.

6. When developing your company, who should be on your core strategic planning team?

Who are the supporters of your self-development? Who is not? Who understands your core values and mirrors them? Who pushes your buttons in ways that make you reach further toward your own unveiling?

These are only suggestions. There are many questions you can ask yourself to fully explore the answer to these questions. Flesh it out, challenge yourself. Let others challenge you.

It's your life...go for it!

16. personal mission statement

What is your code of conduct?
What mark do you want to leave on this earth?

To commence our personal mission statement, we must identify where we want to make room for transition. That is, what is the gap between where we are and where we want to be in accordance with our true selves. Looking at the exercises you have been doing in this journal so far, what would you identify as some of the areas where you want to bridge the gap?

It is in the present moment that each choice is made. How we choose to react depends on our level of focus on past, present and future. Most importantly, true-self or personality will determine any response to stimuli. As we develop the gap between stimulus and response, by being in the *present moment of choice,* we develop character and personality in alignment with our true selves.

MY PERSONAL MISSION STATEMENT

Before my eyes are fully open and ready to see this new day, let me remember these things:

- *When my feet first touch the ground beneath my bed, let me move gracefully toward the things that awaken my capacity to give and receive love.*

- *I chose to live life as though each moment, each experience is neither good nor bad, rather it is an opportunity to discover more about the power of unconditional love.*

- *Fear only limits my ability to see clearly so I choose to face my fears with open eyes and an open heart*

- *I choose to unveil my essence through taking 100% responsibility for my thinking, feelings and actions.*

- *I dedicate my life to living the highest version of the grandest vision of who I am.*

A Daily Reminder of Who You Are

Each day as I wake I remind myself who I am, and what I want to be today.

With all of the world's focus on things that do not relate to who I choose to be,

I must remind myself.

I remember this moment is the only moment I have.

How do I want to experience my family, friends, my self?

How do I want experience all that is offered to me in this day?

How do I want to learn from the people and situations surrounding me today?

How can I make my own learning most enjoyable, kind and respectful?

This reminder is a daily event for those of us choosing to live consciously. We don't wake up one day and suddenly join the "Conscious Club". I believe anyone, and I will be bold in saying "**anyone**" who is serious about using their lives to grow in consciousness, will need to check themselves and where their intention is placed at least several times each day. Depending on the degree we are challenged by the people and situations surrounding us us at the time, we may need to check in moment by moment, second by second! For this reason I have learned to insure I have some love and kindness surrounding me, especially in times when I'm dealing with the opposite.

I know I'm not a saint, and I may experience a little struggle throughout my day; some days more than others. However, now I know ways in which I can be kinder to myself and others in the process, so I still have an opportunity to choose love even for my own fear.

There is a great saying that bounces around business seminars and motivational emails:

"People don't plan to fail,
they fail to plan."

A bank would not lend any business money if it had no plan or direction to follow in order to make lending a successful proposition. What makes us think our lives are so much less important?

LIVE A RIGHT LIFE

I remember hearing a very sad story about a man, who on his death bed said to his elderly wife,

"What if my whole life has been wrong?"

Please don't allow your life to be wrong. Only you can know how to have your right life. The answers are discovered by living each day like you know that it's your last. As you continue to connect to this place, you bridge the gap between who you think you are, and who you truly are.

You are so much more than you might think, and the world is a better place because you are choosing to discover this truth.

EXERCISE 16A

WHAT IS IMPORTANT TO YOU?

Before you create your own personal mission statement (which of course is a work in progress), finishing the following sentences may help you focus on what is most important to you.

1. I know the past does not = the future because…

2. I simply won't compromise…

3. I struggle with my ego the most when…

4. I feel most connected to my spirit when…

5. I want to be a person who…

6. I think the reason I'm here right now on this earth is…

7. I am truly happy when…

8. My deepest joy is experienced when…

9. The most important things are…

10. I really admire and respect   *(person's name)*

because

EXERCISE 16B

OPPORTUNITY TO CREATE YOUR GRANDEST VERSION OF YOU.

One more step before the actual event...

Five minute continuous writing exercise—I use this practice of continuous writing with all of my clients and in almost every workshop I undertake because I never cease to be amazed at what lies within everyone who is willing to let go and simply write whatever comes to them. I have read some of the most profound writings from the most unassuming and remarkable individuals.

I'm reminded of a seminar I conducted just outside Melbourne for a prestigious international car company. When I took fifteen executives into a meditation room that was fully equipped with six foot tall candelabras, floor cushions, burning oils and relaxation music, I think I shocked them right out of their comfortable high-backed office chairs! They giggled like school boys when asked to find a place in the meditation circle. One man was so shy, he hardly spoke a word for the first two days of our conference. He seemed to be enjoying our work together, but his lack of contribution made it difficult for me to gage how much he was taking in, until we did the continuous writing exercise. His words were so powerful and profound I remember having tears rolling down my face as he shared his deepest truth about his highest knowing of who he is within his true-self. His contributions seemed to increase naturally from that moment. I suspected it might have been because until he saw it on paper himself, he had never known that he had all of that wisdom and love to contribute.

Remember to Breathe

I suggest you start by doing a short breathing exercise whenever you want to center yourself. Let go of inhibition and open up to your natural knowledge of who you are.

- Breathe-in with the focus on connecting to that part of yourself and the universe that is all-knowing, gentle, wise and loving.

- Breathe-out with your focus on releasing any blockages that might limit your connection to your inner wisdom.

If words or images which seem unrelated or unusual come to you, write them down anyway. There is only one rule and that is your pen cannot leave the page for five minutes. Set the alarm clock so you don't have to keep looking up at the time and distracting yourself away from your center.

In the back of this book or in your own journal, begin to write now...

My Personal Mission Statement

this dance is just beginning

I have said many times throughout this book that your unique discovery of just how magnificent you really are is a never ending process. I hope these pages have served as a reminder of this truth; however, it is only the beginning.

All the exercises in this book are examples of the many ways in which you can learn to be more in love with yourself and with the world we live in. It can be tough! I urge you to revisit exercises you found helpful. At different times during the unfolding of different "dramas" you might need a reminder. We all do.

Nothing and nobody

can be compared to you...

so share with us your dance.

Please don't feel if you are not absolutely 100% loving, happy, and at peace with the world today that you have in some way failed this process. This is not an audition or a dance competition. It is the ongoing life rehearsal. You cannot be kicked off the stage or voted out because your dance wasn't good enough according to others who for the most part can know only very little about your unique craft. Nobody can judge your dance. That's the beauty of being an individual! There is nothing and nobody who can be compared to you so how can they judge? Where's the benchmark?

It's not over and there is no fat lady to sing. (I never did understand that saying anyway.) There are so many other wonderful sources of inspiration and support that can move with you as you grow. Allow your intuition to guide you to books, inspiration cards, groups, relaxation CDs, friendships, the internet…

There is no limit to the ways in which you can continue to perfect your dance. As you may have worked out by now, when I speak of my dance, I mean my ability to be all that I am and allow others to do the same…with joy and gratitude. In the dance I am learning to love myself and the world in which I live just a little more every day. I've struggled to do that. My experience is that most people do. So I give myself Permission to be human in the process. That for me is the gradual perfecting of my dance.

In "reality", the only dance is love.

I don't want to miss out on one tiny step!

Who says life isn't a dress rehearsal?

I hope for your sake you will allow life to be your very own dress
rehearsal. Perhaps if we could all let go of the notion that life is a
show that must go on, and of course one where looking good and
putting on a good performance are considered more important
than feeling whole; maybe then we could more easily give
ourselves Permission to use this lifetime as a stage where our soul
evolves through varied scenes playing out.

You are the star of your show.
You choose who dances on your stage and for how long.

I hope you will be kind to yourself and others as we all fall down
and get back up again.

my wish for us

May we dance in the rhythm of our own heartbeat

And in that movement discover our greatest potential.

May we remember that we are all doing our best

When we know better we do better.

May we find our heart more open

Our hands more willing

like children, fearless and eager to explore.

We are the One Family of Earth

May we learn to dance as one body

To sing in one song

And to love . . .

Especially may we love.

I thank each and every one of you for this dance—without you, there would have been no book written, no seminars in which to see your beautiful faces, and no dance partners in which to share this song that comes from a place within. My humanness yearned to share it.

I wish that you might choose to fly higher than your imagination has ever dared to soar; that you make it your business to be unlimited… and I wish that you might remember to dance as if this moment is your last!

Until we meet again…

Gayla.

Keep your eyes open, you are being lavished with gifts!

Laugh more.

Struggle less.

And always remember to dance!

P.S. No need to dance alone . . .

There are many wonderful teachers who come in all forms. Trust your inner guidance and be aware that as you are lead to the right support for right now, they will also be blessed by the lessons you provide them. My way of doing things is not everyone's way. Let that be what it is and move in your own rhythm, trusting you will find others who will serve to be your perfect teachers, guides and of course at the same time, also your students.

Today I

give myself
Permission to
Practice life to
the fullest...

Today I

REMEMBER THERE

IS NOBODY MORE

WORTHY OF MY LOVE

AND COMPASSION

THAN ME...

Today I

I give myself
Permission to try
something new…
and not be absolutely
perfect at it yet!

today I

I choose to focus on

what is going well in

my life, in my family

and in the world…

Today I

feel
grateful
for the
smallest
things...

Today I

trust all is

in perfect

order...

Today I

acknowledge my uniqueness and allow others to do the same...

PERMISSION TO PRACTICE this dance is just the beginning

Today I

remember how tricky
my ego can be and I
am gentle on myself
and others as I witness
it in action…

Today I

focus on
bringing my
thoughts back
to Love rather
than fear

Today

Practice exposes

my perfection.

Today I choose to

focus on enjoying

the ME I see!

Big Thanks!

To my clients who have trusted' shared and allowed me to witness their transformations. You bring these truths to life as I am honored to witness love in action every day I'm working with you.

Gayla.

About the Author

Gayla Maxwell was born in Canada and has made Australia her home since 1980.

She is a writer, clinical hypnotherapist and creative performance consultant; her work focusing on emotional wellbeing, and the power that unfolds when we discover the fullness of *who we are most naturally*. Gayla teaches that we are all natural creators in some way but we have been conditioned subconsciously to live in fear and self-doubt, which can be overcome.

Gayla has been a Master Trainer in suicide prevention, providing training to psychologists, general practitioners, teachers, and anyone working with people at risk of suicidal ideation. During that time she became aware of the need to design preventative programs, focusing more on emotional fitness and less on mental illness.

With a natural passion and empathy for who she calls 'the sensitive creatives', Gayla has taken her skills and knowledge of subconscious mind techniques to specialize in coaching actors, musicians and others in the creative arts industries. She has been empowering anyone seeking to overcome limiting self-doubt so they are able to access a deeper level of self- expression, while having more grounded, healthy relationships with themselves and the world around them.

Gayla now spends most of her time writing, mentoring and hanging out with her best friends Bob the scruffy poodle and Bruce the bossy black cat.

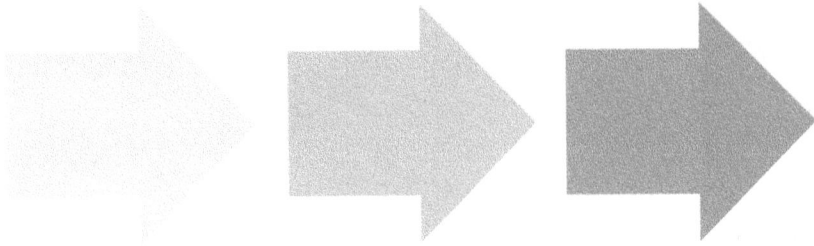

Dedication

To my wise mother, who often said, *'My dear daughter, you are far too tough on yourself'*. The exercises in these pages wouldn't have been written without my own effort to undo this true statement.

To my beautiful sister Donna, who taught me the importance of truly living each moment because her moments were taken from her too young.

To my gentle father, who chose me, and loved me as his own, when he didn't have to. His quiet manner was my drinking well of stability, safety and comfort.

To my Tour Guide, who is an eternal voice in my head, still reminding me to give *myself* permission to dance.

I feel each of you around me, still guiding me. I'm eternally grateful.

"Isn't it liberating knowing we are not only allowed to be all that we are, but in fact without us BEING that, the world misses out on the chain of events which are a result of our every mishap and our beautiful triumphs.

It is all designed so perfectly I can only **try to imagine."**

This place isn't the same without you.

IF YOU DON'T FALL DOWN MUCH, YOU PROBABLY HAVEN'T LEARNED MUCH.

welcome to
the beginning...

www.ingramcontent.com/pod-product-compliance
Lightning Source LLC
Chambersburg PA
CBHW080249030426

42334CB00023BA/2753

* 9 780987 228628 *